DEMAND DYNAMICS

THE FORCES OF DEMAND IN GLOBAL SEX TRAFFICKING

CONFERENCE REPORT

Conference held October 17 and 18, 2003

Chicago, Illinois, USA

Morrison Torrey, General Editor

Sara Dubin, Student Reporter Editor

Organized by Captive Daughters and

the International Human Rights Law Institute,

DePaul University College of Law

International Human Rights Law Institute

In 1990, the International Human Rights Law Institute was established within DePaul University College of Law in response to sweeping global changes that created new opportunities to advance human rights and strengthen domestic and international legal institutions. The Institute is dedicated to developing and promoting international human rights law and international criminal justice through fieldwork, research, documentation, publications, and advocacy.

This publication has been generously underwritten by **The Jeanne and Joseph Sullivan Human Rights Program in the Americas**.

The ideas and opinions of conference participants contained in this report are not necessarily those of Captive Daughters or the International Human Rights Law Institute.

Printed in the United States of America.

ISBN 1-889001-06-6

TABLE OF CONTENTS

Conference Schedule

Demand Dynamics
The Forces of Demand in
Global Sex Trafficking

Welcome & Introductions
Sandra Hunnicutt, Captive Daughters
Morrison Torrey, DePaul University College of Law
Michelle Dempsey, Conference Moderator
Kaethe Morris Hoffer, Conference Spokesperson
M. Cherif Bassiouni, IHRLI President

Keynote Address
*Dorchen Leidholdt, D*irector, Center for Battered Women's Legal Ser-
vices, Sanctuary for Families; Co- Director, Coalition Against
Trafficking in Women

**Panel 1: What do we know about the people who make up the "de-
mand" side of sex trafficking?**

Moderator
Kristen Houser, Nebraska Domestic Violence Sexual Assault Coalition

Panelists
Melissa Farley, Prostitution Research, San Francisco, CA
Stephen Grubman-Black, University of Rhode Island
Mary Anne Layden, University of Pennsylvania Health Systems
Brenda Myers, Chicago Coalition for the Homeless

Panel 2: How do consumers of sex trafficking find their "supply," and how is demand manipulated and maintained?

Moderator
Laura Lederer, United States Department of State

Panelists
Derek Ellerman, Polaris Project
Jackson Katz, MVP Strategies
Marisa Ugarte, Bilateral Safety Corridor Coalition

Panel 3: What governmental policies or practices enable the actions of those who create demand?

Moderator
Vidyamali Samarasinghe, American University, Washington, DC

Panelists
Kenneth Franzblau, Equality Now, New York
Donna Hughes, University of Rhode Island

Film
Diane Rosenfeld, Women's Studies, Harvard University, and co-producer of the film *Rape Is...,* a half-hour documentary exploring the meaning and consequences of rape and discussing the relationship between rape, sex trafficking, and prostitution.

Panel 4: What can be done to interfere with and ultimately eliminate demand?

Moderator
Normal Hotaling, Standing Against Global Exploitation (SAGE)

Panelists
Margaret Baldwin, Florida State University
Mohamed Mattar, Protection Project, Johns Hopkins University
Pamela Shifman, UNICEF

Plenary Session: Plan for Action
Moderators
Pamela Shifman, UNICEF
Morrison Torrey, DePaul University College of Law

Note: Panels 1 and 2 are reversed from their actual presentation, which had been scheduled to accommodate panelists.

Conference Organizers

Captive Daughters is the first anti-trafficking group established in California. We focus solely on ending the sexual bondage of female adolescents and children. The organization was inspired by the founding director's stay in Nepal, where she learned firsthand about sexual trafficking. Upon returning to the United States in 1995, she began researching trafficking and discovered a fragile network of groups struggling to educate the public on trafficking both here and abroad. In an effort to strengthen that movement, she and a committed group of individuals established Captive Daughters as a non-profit organization in 1997.

As a founding principle, Captive Daughters holds that the practice of sex trafficking is a direct assault on the basic human rights and lives of female children. While recognizing that sex trafficking is a violation of fundamental human rights that profoundly effects the lives and welfare of both women and children, Captive Daughters has chosen to focus its efforts on combating sex trafficking particularly as it affects girls and adolescent females. Our goal is to bring public attention to and call for the elimination of their forced prostitution. We seek to encourage national and international attention to sex trafficking by informing the general public about the scope and severity of the problem. To accomplish this, we share information via our website, participate in national and international forums and media outreach, collaborate with sister organizations, and encourage the television, film, publishing, and artistic communities to focus on sex-trafficking in their work.

Sandra Hunnicut,
Captive Daughters
10410 Palms Blvd., Box 22
Los Angeles, CA 90034

The International Human Rights Law Institute of DePaul University College of Law was established in 1990 within the College of Law at DePaul University in response to sweeping global changes that created new opportunities to advance human rights and strengthen domestic and international legal institutions. The Institute is dedicated to developing and promoting international human rights law and international criminal justice through fieldwork, research, documentation, publications, advocacy, and technical legal assistance to governments and non-governmental organizations. It also trains new generations of human rights advocates.

In 1998, the Institute initiated a project on worldwide trafficking in women and children for purposes of exploitation. Based upon this initial work, the Institute then joined with the Inter-American Commission on Women, the Inter- American Commission on Children, and the Organization of American States (along with other collaborators) to conduct the first regional empirical study of this problem in the Americas. Field research was conducted in eight countries in Central America, the Caribbean, and in Brazil. The results of this study were published at the end of 2002 and in early 2003.

International Human Rights Law Institute
DePaul University College of Law
25 East Jackson Blvd.,
Chicago, IL 60604

Preface

The seed for "Demand Dynamics" was planted in 2002, as we prepared to write Captive Daughters' year-end letter to our supporters. As usual, the letter covered our accomplishments during the past year and our goals for the coming year. During a discussion of ideas for projects in 2003, I suggested convening a fall conference on trafficking in Chicago, where I once lived. The Captive Daughters Board said it sounded like a good idea. For an all-volunteer group, it would be a huge undertaking; it would be great if we pulled it off, but no one would fault us if it proved too much. Our letter went out in November, and I pretty much let the idea go.

Then, in December of 2002, I attended "Protecting Our Children," a conference hosted by the Office of Juvenile Justice & Delinquency Prevention. At the end of the conference, I overheard people saying, "but they didn't really talk about demand! When are we going to hear more about demand?" Two months later, I attended a State Department conference, "Pathbreaking Strategies in the Global Fight against Sex Trafficking," which included a 90-minute workshop on demand for a specific group of attendees. Again, I heard people complaining: "we need to have more time for demand than a workshop." At that moment, I knew we had our conference topic.

Many people came forward to help craft the conference outline: Matt Friedman of USAID, then stationed in Bangladesh; Michelle Dempsey in London; and Lisa Kelly of Captive Daughters in Los Angeles. During one e-mail discussion, Michelle suggested that we approach the International Human Rights Law Institute (IHRLI) at DePaul University College of Law to see if they would be interested in co-sponsoring the still unnamed conference. When I approached David Guinn, Executive Director of IHRLI, he agreed that the demand topic had never been addressed sufficiently and committed to co-sponsor the conference. Shortly after that, we had a steering committee, a title, a compelling conference outline, and a lot of work to do. Captive Daughters is indebted to IHRLI for taking a leap of faith and believing that a tiny, all-volunteer organization could make "Demand Dynamics" happen.

And it did happen, mostly through a constant flood of e-mails between Los Angeles, Chicago, and London. Not one Captive Daughters board member or volunteer had ever helped create a national conference, but with the support of our co-hosts in Chicago, we learned. We were challenged plenty of times along the way, particularly in the area of funding. We approached many foundations, but none offered assistance. Because foundations have yet to recognize the scope of sex trafficking and its impact at the health and human services levels, they do not understand the importance of funding education, research, and prevention. Fortunately, several individuals and faith-based organizations provided financial support, and they are gratefully included in our Acknowledgments section.

This conference has created much interest around the world. We look forward to seeing how our Action Plan will be implemented and welcome announcements of other demand-related conferences. We hope to see increased funding for research on demand and for NGOs working on demand-related projects. We are particularly pleased that DePaul created the first comprehensive demand bibliography in the United States.

Captive Daughters is committed to focusing on the demand issue in our work. We invite you to join us in our effort to combat those who sexually exploit women and children.

Sandra Hunnicutt
Executive Director,
Captive Daughters

The IHRLI enthusiastically embraced the idea of co-sponsoring this important conference with Captive Daughters, an NGO committed to fighting international sex trafficking. Since 1998, the Institute has been examining the international trafficking of women and children for sexual exploitation within a human rights framework. Because of its previous involvement in human rights work in the Americas, in 2000 the IHRLI initially focused these research efforts on Latin America and the Caribbean. The Institute published its findings in October 2002 in *In Modern Bondage: Sex Trafficking in the Americas (Central America and the Caribbean)* (copies available from IHRLI, ihrli@depaul.edu). From the beginning, however, the IHRLI has recognized that demand drives the trade in women and children's bodies. This was acknowledged in its 2002 report:

> The root cause of trafficking is demand for commercial sexual services, without which trafficking for purposes of sexual exploitation would dissolve. The demand connected to trafficking in the region [Central America and the Caribbean] is predominately for prostitution and stripping. While some advocacy groups, most notably *Casa Alianza*, have investigated and denounced pedophiles, child pornography rings and internet sites promoting the sexual exploitation of minors, the information available does not yet draw a clear line of connection between trafficking activity and the production of pornographic materials in the region.
>
> Demand within the region is concentrated in "zones of tolerance," tourist areas, ports, along international trucking routes, and in certain agricultural areas where migrant laborers are predominately male. The growth of the tourism industry and the increasing number of gambling establishments in the region have also opened markets for the industry. Varying forms of prostitution also occur in public markets and border areas. Bar owners, taxi drivers, hotel managers, market vendors, and independent pimps all serve the demands of clients.

In Modern Bondage at 45. The Demand Dynamics Conference is an important step in addressing issues concerning demand and its elimination.

Professor Morrison Torrey
International Human
Rights Law Institute

Acknowledgements

We gratefully acknowledge the support of David Guinn, Executive Director of IHRLI, during the organizing phase of this Conference as well as for securing the funds to publish this Conference Report.

When we decided to publish a Conference Report, it seemed essential to make a record of the proceedings that would include question and answer segments as well as the presentations by panelists who did not submit written remarks. The solution, seeking student reporters, also provided opportunities for DePaul University College of Law students to participate in and contribute to the Conference. These student reporters did a wonderfully professional job and are acknowledged in the text for the specific summaries and materials they provided; however, we want to particularly express our appreciation to Christine Shepard, Kirstie Bowling, Shelly Geppert, Amany Ezeldin, Gil Lenz, Heena Musabji, Jamie Sommer, Sarah James, Pavana Bhat, and Rima Kapitan. DePaul Law students Laura Pichardo and Kate Dailey volunteered as videocamera operators to record the Conference. Additionally, several DePaul Law School Alumni, namely Jaime Olson, Carol Chang, and Ling Chin, volunteered in various capacities. DePaul Law School staff Cora Malinak and Lawrence Arendt have also contributed generously their time and effort to the Conference and this Report. We also want to thank DePaul Law Students who acted as press aides: Pavana Bhat, Michael Blankenheim, and Sara James. And, of course, a great deal of gratitude goes to Heena Musabji for researching and compiling the bibliography. Finally, the Conference Report would never had made it to publication without the editing and proofreading skills of Meredith Barges.

Other people provided services and support in multiple ways: Terry Phillips of Soroptimist Clubs organized a Soroptomist Reception for speakers and participants in the Conference and Valerie Phillips, DePaul University Media Relations Specialist, helped to get the word out to various media outlets. The staff at Newberry Library, site of the Conference, was wonderful, especially Karen Skubish and Karen Smith.

Captive Daughters wishes to acknowledge the dedication and support of the following people in making Demand Dynamics a success: Sara Dubin, Kaethe Morris Hoffer, Lisa Kelly, Michelle Madden Dempsey, and Morrison Torrey, as well as a heartfelt thank you to board members Ken Lee, Stephen Long, Yosh Yamanaka, and Hanna Zylberberg.

And, finally, Demand Dynamics never would have happened without the vision, energy, and commitment of Sandra Hunnicutt.

Keynote Address:
Demand and the Debate

Dorchen A. Leidholdt

It is a tremendous honor to be speaking here. And a little daunting. When I looked at the list of participants, I saw the names of so many people I have worked with since the '70s and 80s in the movement against prostitution and pornography. So many people who have raised my consciousness and taught me unforgettable lessons are here– Meg Baldwin, Twiss Butler, Melissa Farley, Ruchira Gupta, Norma Hotaling, Donna Hughes, Laura Lederer, Linnea Smith, Morrison Torrey, and many others here. It is a privilege to be here with you. And what a pleasure and relief not to have to try to convince another audience that trafficking and prostitution harm women.

I'd like to talk about our history–the journey, politically speaking, that has brought us to this conference. It's a collective history, but we've had different experiences–we have different battle scars, different successes. I'd like to speak personally, about my experience in this movement and in the debate that has brought us to this conference. And I'd like to explain how, in my view, the subject we are focusing on at this conference–the demand for commercial sexual exploitation–helps resolve the debate and enables us to make a real difference in stopping the commercial sexual exploitation of women and children.

I first encountered the debate in 1978. I was part of a little cadre of feminist activists in New York City who made up the NYC groups of Women Against Violence Against Women, or WAVAW, as it was called. WAVAW was working against images in the popular media that eroticized and promoted violence against women. I was also working with New York Women Against Rape.

In the fall of 1977, there was an incident that stunned and galvanized us. A young woman was thrown out of the window of a building onto the pavement below. She was brutally murdered. But because she was in prostitution and the window was that of a brothel, the police were not taking her murder seriously. She was, as the media put it, "a hooker." We were outraged. We called an emergency meeting. We spray painted signs that communicated our anger. I typed up a leaflet and used the xerox machine of the publishing company where I worked to run off hundreds of copies. This woman was our sister, we declared, and her murder was a crime against all women. We sent out a press release to announce that we would be picketing in front of the brothel.

WAVAW and New York Women Against Rape were not the only groups to show up, however. Members of another group were there. They were British-based and called themselves Wages for Housework. Whereas our message was simple and feminist, theirs was more sophisticated and complex. The media turned out in droves, and our Wages for Housework comrades hogged the microphones.

"Prostitution is a job like any other job," they insisted. "Some women prostitute their fingers as secretaries; others prostitute their minds as college professors."

"It's all the same."

"If we unionized brothels and recognized sex work as a job, this never would have happened."

"There's no difference between prostitution and marriage: hookers and housewives unite."

I was impressed by the glibness of the Wages for Housework activists, I admired their media savvy, and I was more than a little intimidated by their aggressiveness. They took over our protest and drowned out our message. But their basic argument didn't ring true for me. I had never heard of a single instance in which a secretary or college professor had been flung out of a window of her workplace to her death on the streets below. And while married women were leaving abusive homes in droves, their prostituted sisters often didn't have homes to leave. It would be six years before I would encounter the Canadian Report on Prostitution and Pornography with its finding that prostituted women in Canada suffer a mortality rate 40 times the national average. But it was no secret that prostituted women were the special targets of serial killers. How many jobs had murder as a frequent workplace safety hazard?

2

The Wages for Housework advocates had borrowed their philosophy from the San Francisco-based organization, COYOTE, an acronym for "Call Off Your Old Tired Ethics." Founded in 1973, COYOTE was made up of a mix of libertarian activists and sex industry profiteers. In 1974, they organized the First Hookers Ball and, two years later, the first Hookers Convention. Both were promotional events backed by the San Francisco sex industry. The public face of COYOTE was Margo St. James, who began her public appearances with the announcement, "I'm a whore." The pimps and pornographers behind the venture laid low. The term, "sex worker," was coined by COYOTE stalwart Priscilla Alexander, who argued with a straight face that her four years at Bennington College qualified her to claim that label.

St. James and Alexander traveled through Western Europe, promoting their philosophy and nomenclature. COYOTE provided the increasingly lucrative European sex industry and the other interests that benefited from it with just the rationale they needed. COYOTE solidified its European base through the First and Second International Whores' Congresses, held in Amsterdam in 1985 and Brussels in 1986.

At the same time that COYOTE was promoting the sex industry, American feminists were organizing to fight it. A 1978 Hustler Magazine cover showed a woman's body being fed through a meat grinder. It forced feminists to confront the sex industry's public relations arm—pornography. Significantly, the feminist movement against pornography was a movement against demand. We made connections between men's demand for and socialization through pornography and the rape, woman battering, and sexual harassment we had begun to mobilized against a decade earlier. We took to the streets with signs that declared, "Pornography is Rape on Paper."

Although many of us believed that we were protesting images of violence, in reality we were protesting violence documented. The rape was not only on paper. The images were mostly photographs of actual women, with histories of horrific abuse, whose bodies were bought, sold, and violated for the benefit of sex industry profiteers. I learned this when, as a spokesperson for Women Against Pornography, I responded to media requests for debates. Usually it wasn't the pornographers we were asked to debate but the women who fronted for them. The media preferred "cat fights," and the pornographers were happy to accommodate them.

3

In the December 1984 issue of Film Comment, I wrote about three of these women: a former "porn star" and so-called producer of a pornography magazine, who struggled to support her daughter and confided to me that her career in the sex industry had been precipitated by a brutal gang rape; a 23-year-old centerfold model with a shattered nose (shattered by a baseball bat), married to a pornographic film director who always kept her in his sights; and another "porn star" who deviated from her script on the air to mention that her husband beat her. I later learned he also pimped her. It was a sobering revelation: the sex industry defenders we were pitted against on TV talk shows were the most brutalized sex industry victims.

Linda Marchiano, pimped, threatened, and beaten by the vicious Chuck Traynor, who, in classic pimp fashion, renamed her Linda Lovelace, was handed a script by her captor: "Q: Does it bother you to suck cock in front of so many people? A: Oh no, I love it. I guess I'm what you call an exhibitionist."

Anneka DiLorenzo, a Penthouse Pet, was sent out on the road by Bob Guccione, publisher of Penthouse, as a "Woman for Pornography." She later successfully sued Guccione for sexual harassment after she proved that he pimped her to a business associate.

But for me, the most profound revelation came not from our opponents but from one of the women in our group. She was a bundle of contradictions: a brilliant feminist theorist and a working class housewife from Queens, trying without success to have a baby. She rose to a leadership position in WAP, and we became close friends. Then I learned why she couldn't have a baby. She had been in prostitution from the time she had run away from her sexually abusive stepfather at age 14 until, her body ravaged by heroin, she was no longer a marketable commodity. Repeated bouts of venereal disease had destroyed her reproductive system. She had scars on her thighs from the time one of her pimps beat her with a coat hanger. She had teeth knocked out from another beating. I had taught Sarah about feminist theory; now she taught me about the lives of women and girls in prostitution. They were lessons that changed my life.

I began to understand, through my work with Sarah, that prostitution was not a job at all. The money it generated rarely ended up in the pocket of the prostituted girl or woman. It usually was confiscated by one of a series of men who pulled her into prostitution and kept her there, often at first through coercion, but later by the creation of an en-

4

vironment that made the batterer's dominion of power and control look like child's play. Worn down by abuse and degradation, she finally submitted to her fate—and that submission was called consent or choice.

As a young feminist in the early 1970s, I had worked as a rape crisis counselor. Now I began to understand that what those women had endured as a one-time assault was the ongoing condition of women and girls in prostitution—a prolonged, numbing series of sexual violations carried out by multiple violators. And this was being done to women and girls, the vast majority of whom had already endured sexual abuse as children. "Sarah" called prostitution "bought and sold rape." But in reality, it was gang rape, and not just a single gang rape, but gang rape carried out day after day for years. The money exchanged—which sex industry defenders pointed to as proof that prostitution is work—only deepened the violation to the woman or girl and her feelings of culpability. I became convinced that the labor paradigm COYOTE and Wages for Housework was promoting was wrong, and that, like rape, prostitution was a practice of gender-based violence.

Sarah left Women Against Pornography to found the first organization of prostitution survivors to fight the sex industry. I wanted also to challenge it—not just the pornography it produced—but working now with Kathleen Barry, the author of *Female Sexual Slavery*, I was thinking globally.

In 1987, colleagues from Women Against Pornography and the Minneapolis-based WHISPER and I began to organize a conference entitled, "Trafficking in Women." I articulated the primary goal of the conference in a letter to Twiss Butler in January 1988: "What we hope to accomplish is to get feminists and others to rethink pornography and prostitution issues from the vantage point of the women who are most victimized by the institutions and simultaneously flaunted and made invisible."

The conference took place in October 1988, one week short of fifteen years ago, in Martin Luther King, Jr. High School in New York City. It was the first international conference on trafficking in women. Laura Lederer, a leader in the anti-pornography movement, was now a program officer at the Skaggs Foundation. Laura provided the seed money that made the conference possible. It was organized on a shoestring, but, without Laura's critical support, it would not have been possible.

Speakers included the founding mothers of the global movement against the sexual exploitation of women, in addition to Kathy Barry and Diana Russell, international leaders like Yayori Matsui, the Japanese feminist extraordinaire and founder of the Asian Women's Association, who tragically died this year; Jyotsna Chatterji, the director of the Joint Women's Programme in New Delhi, India; Agnete Strom of the Women's Front in Norway; Aurora Javate de Dios, the director of the Women's Resource and Research Center in the Philippines; Rosa Dominga-Trapasso, founder of the Movimeiento el Pozo in Peru; British lesbian-feminist author and anti-pornography activist Sheila Jeffreys; and Zimbabwe's leading women's rights scholar Rudo Gaidzanwa. Survivors participated on panels and in a three-hour speak out.

The conference organizers understood trafficking in women as a broad umbrella concept that encompassed all practices of buying and selling women's and children's bodies. Trafficking, as we understood it, included American pornography, temple prostitution in India, military prostitution in the Philippines, street prostitution in Peru, and sex tourism from Europe to Asia. It moved from the micro-"Trafficking within the Family" to the macro-"Trafficking in Women: A Global Perspective." It exposed mainstream institutions that support and benefit from prostitution: "Military, Government, and Corporate Trafficking in Women." The conference looked at the sex industry as an instrument of the socialization of both men and women: "The Social Production of Prostitution"; and "On Sale Everywhere: The Social Reconstruction of Women's Bodies." It exposed connections between sex trafficking and surrogacy, marriage, and adoption. It focused on violence against prostitutes, called for services and shelter for victims and survivors, and examined international legal strategies on trafficking in women.

Please forgive me if I dwell on the content of the conference, but I just received a program for a conference on human trafficking that will soon take place in New York City. You would never know that trafficking has anything to do with gender, sex, or women.

It was clear by the end of the conference that an international feminist organization combating trafficking in women, in all of its forms, was desperately needed. We began organizing the Coalition Against Trafficking in Women. Many of the conference participants took on key roles. Aurora Javate de Dios from the Philippines became our President.

6

We conceived of the Coalition as an umbrella with connected but autonomous networks in each world region to address its unique challenges. Within the next five years, there was a strong Coalition Against Trafficking in Women, Asia-Pacific, with Aurora at the helm; a newly formed Coalition Against Trafficking in Women, Latin America, coordinated by Zoraida Ramirez Rodriquez in Venezuela, whom we lost to breast cancer last year; and an incipient African Coalition being developed by Fatoumata Diake in Mali.

Not everyone was happy with the inclusive and feminist understanding of trafficking that was promoted at the 1988 Conference and embraced by the Coalition Against Trafficking in Women. Representatives from the Center for Women's Global Leadership observed the proceedings without participating, whispering among themselves. Representatives from the Dutch Foundation on Trafficking in Women arrived uninvited and did their best to foster dissent among the participants. However, it was not until 1991 during a seminar on trafficking in women in Strasbourg, France, sponsored by the Council of Europe and the Dutch government, that the opposition's agenda and strategy fully surfaced.

I flew into Frankfurt on my way to Strasbourg, and used that opportunity to study, up close, legalized prostitution, European-style. The Frankfurt city fathers had created a system of legal, regulated brothels, hoping to stamp out an array of evils, including street prostitution, control of the sex industry by organized crime, and the spread of sexually transmitted diseases. It was obvious that their strategy was a colossal failure. Street prostitution was flourishing; organized crime groups were running underground brothels filled with Asian, Latin American, and Eastern European women and girls. Only the few legal brothels (grossly out numbered by their underground counterparts) cared whether buyers used condoms.

What had emerged in Frankfurt was a two-tiered system of prostitution. I later realized that this was the face of legalized prostitution in the western world. Women and girls who had been trafficked from poor countries were propelled into competition with Western-born women for local prostitution customers and a growing number of sex tourists. It was apparent that the quotient of suffering was most acute for the undocumented women and girls in the illegal brothels. They were forced to endure unwanted sex with half-a-dozen customers each night, were unable to protect themselves from HIV and other sexually

7

transmitted diseases, and were deprived of travel documents, threatened with violence and deportation, and required to work off exorbitant debt that locked them into conditions of slavery.

While not as dire as that of their internationally trafficked sisters, the lot of the legally prostituted women was also dismal. Posing as an American newspaper reporter, I was welcomed by the madam into a legal brothel in the heart of Frankfurt. It resembled a four-star hotel in the United States. I was soon surrounded by a group of women eager for a distraction from their late afternoon wait for their "clients." Several of the women's husbands were also their pimps, most of the women were from poor, rural areas of Germany, and all faced bleak futures with few employment skills. The sex act of prostitution was an unwanted invasion that the prostituted women had developed a series of strategies to avoid–their favorite, they confided, was to get the men so drunk that they didn't know what they were penetrating. The women seemed bored and depressed. Their depression deepened when I asked them what they hoped to be doing in five years. Aside from one woman who said that she hoped to help manage the brothel, they were at a loss for words.

The effects of trafficking and prostitution were not confined to the brothels in Frankfurt. I was told by Asian women working to assist trafficking victims that they couldn't publish their names in the telephone books or they got calls all night long from prostitution buyers. They were constantly solicited for sex. The mainstream media was saturated with prostitution imagery.

When I boarded the train to Strasbourg, it seemed indisputable to me that prostitution and sex trafficking were interrelated phenomena. Once I arrived at my destination, however, the conference organizers– the Dutch government-funded Foundation Against Trafficking– announced that they thought otherwise. All of the participants were instructed that the conference was about trafficking; prostitution was not to be discussed. As the conference proceeded, it became clear that the organizers had developed an extremely narrow definition of trafficking: the coerced transport of people across national or regional boundaries. The fact that women were trafficked for the purpose of prostitution was, to the organizers, irrelevant. It was irrelevant that the women were trafficked into brothels and strip clubs; their focus was exclusively confined to international criminal networks forcibly moving people across borders.

8

It became evident that the conference organizers' circumscribed definition of trafficking and their censorship of the topic of prostitution were a deliberate strategy. The Dutch government, which had funded the conference, was convinced that the sex industry can be a safe and lucrative source of income for countries and women alike if prostitution is legalized and regulated. All of the abuses apparent in local and global sex industries, they argued, derive from their illegal status, which drives them underground and under the control of organized crime. Prostitution, if made legal and cleansed of its stigma, can be a job like any other job, echoing the words of COYOTE.

A decade after the conference, the Dutch government fully implemented its agenda by legalizing and licensing 2,000 brothels and registering as prostitutes the women and girls in them. Once prostitution was legal in the Netherlands, brothel owners began to recruit women into prostitution through government-sponsored job centers for unemployed workers.

The conference organizers' efforts to censor discussion about prostitution backfired. Several of the participants insisted on addressing it. One of the dissenting voices was that of Swedish social work professor Sven Axel Manson, who had conducted studies of male prostitution customers and was convinced that trafficking could not be curtailed without strong measures to confront and eliminate the demand for prostituted women and girls. To my immense relief, a handful of us, including an intrepid octogenarian abolitionist, Denise Pouillon, spoke out, pointing to the connections between prostitution and trafficking, and, if only for the moment, derailing the conference organizers' agenda.

The pro-prostitution lobby regrouped. By October 1994, there was an international organization working on the issue of trafficking from "a prostitution is work" perspective–the Global Alliance Against Trafficking in Women or GAATW for short. Today, if you go to the GAATW website, based in Thailand, and follow the chain of links, you end up back at the very place our journey began–the San Francisco sex industry and COYOTE. By the latter half of the 1990s, GAATW was joined by the International Human Rights Law Group.

Where the Coalition defined trafficking to encompass the widest array of practices of commercial sexual exploitation, GAATW and its allies narrowed "trafficking" to the movement of forced or deceived people across borders. As Evelina Giobbe declared in a 1999 debate between the Coalition and GAATW: "You would think from that the problem isn't trafficking–it's traveling."

The Coalition made connections between the private violence of incest, rape, and spousal abuse and the public violence of commercial sexual exploitation; between local prostitution businesses and the global sex industry; between the condition of prostituted women and the status of all women. GAATW and its allies eschewed such analysis. In its lexicon, the term prostitution was replaced by "forced prostitution," which suggested that prostitution is problematic only when coerced. Then, perhaps in an effort to shield the institution of prostitution from any unpleasant associations, the word "prostitution" disappeared from their discourse entirely, replaced by "sex work." "Sex trafficking" was replaced by "facilitated migration" or "human trafficking."

Soon references to "women and girls" and "gender and sex" began to disappear. In March of this year, I participated in a panel in which a representative from a GAATW-affiliated NGO gave a presentation on "human trafficking." You would never know from her remarks that women are trafficked in the millions for exploitation in prostitution. She never once referred to sexual exploitation. Indeed, you would think from her remarks that women and men suffer identical, gender-neutral harm in trafficking: the harm of being deceived or forced into exploitative labor.

In 1998, the International Labor Organization published a pamphlet entitled, "The Sex Sector," that called for the legitimization of the sex industry and argued that sex industry profits should be factored into national accounting schemes. When the Coalition slammed the ILO for promoting prostitution as work, the agency took a different tack. This year, ILO has a new report on trafficking that insists that labor trafficking is the real problem and that sex trafficking is of comparatively minor significance.

Clearly, being trafficked into exploitative farm or factory work is incompatible with fundamental human rights and is harmful to those who are subjected to this form of trafficking. But is that harm really as severe as the harm to women and girls trafficked into prostitution in brothels and over and over again subjected to intimate violation–to rape? Also ignored is the fact that trafficking for purposes of labor exploitation is different for men and women–it is gendered. Women who are trafficked into exploitative factory or domestic work often suffer sexual exploitation by employers and their agents. It is supremely ironic that at a time when international agencies are hiring gender consultants to conduct gender analyses, organizations that are ostensibly fighting trafficking are deliberately ignoring the uniquely gender-based harm of trafficking in women. It is more than ironic–it represents a backlash against feminism and makes a mockery of human rights activism!

The drafters of the United Nations' Convention for the Suppression of the Traffic in Persons and of the Exploitation of Prostitution of Others (the "1949 Convention") did not find it necessary to define trafficking. They understood trafficking to be a cross-border practice of "the exploitation of the prostitution of others" and drafted a treaty that addressed both human rights violations equally. Together, as they understood it, "trafficking in persons and the exploitation of the prostitution of others" encompasses the activities of an increasingly global sex industry whose activities were "incompatible with the dignity and worth of the human person" (Marcovich, 2002). In 1979, the drafters of the Convention on the Elimination of All Forms of Discrimination Against Women (CEDAW) embraced the language of the 1949 Convention, its Article 6 requiring States Parties to "take all appropriate measures, including legislation, to suppress all forms of traffic in women and exploitation of the prostitution of women."

A perceived need to define trafficking and to distinguish it from prostitution came only much later in the 1980s. The goal was to confine both the scope of domestic and international laws addressing the sex industry and activism against it. The 1949 Convention criminalized the profit-making activities of local and global sex industries without penalizing those exploited in prostitution. Had the Convention been equipped with implementing mechanisms that enforced its provisions, it would have posed a serious threat to sex industry businesses. An international movement to abolish prostitution, founded by Josephine Butler at the end of the Nineteenth Century, was still active in the 1980s, and feminists speaking out against the sexual exploitation of women in prostitution were beginning to join forces with the "abolitionists" to strengthen the 1949 Convention and to pass and implement national and local laws consistent with it. Media reports of the suffering of trafficking victims and the increasing globalization of the sex industry were fueling support for a campaign against the sex industry. Eager to ward off such a danger, pro-sex industry forces developed a strategy.

Ignoring or denying the harm of the sex industry was not an option, for that harm was well documented. A more pragmatic approach was to focus on the most brutal and extreme practices of the sex industry–transporting women from poor countries to rich countries using tactics of debt bondage and overt force–while legitimizing its other activities in the name of workers' rights.

The battle over definitions of trafficking came to a fore in 1999 in the drafting of the Trafficking Protocol to the Transnational Convention Against Organized Crime. Several mainstream human rights organizations led by the International Human Rights Law Group supported a definition of trafficking that required proof of force and deceit. Explicitly feminist human rights groups–most prominently the Coalition Against Trafficking in Women, Equality Now, and the European Women's Lobby–called for a definition of trafficking that at a minimum included trafficking carried out by the abuse of a position of power or a situation of vulnerability. In this international context, where developing countries grappling with the devastation wrought by the sex industry were active participants, the arguments of the pro-prostitution lobby foundered, and the more inclusive and protective definition won.

In contrast, that same year, Congress passed the Trafficking Victims Protection Act. Its provisions governing the penalization of traffickers and the protection of victims were limited to cases of "severe trafficking," requiring proof that the trafficking was carried out by force or deceit. Although such a restrictive definition creates an often insurmountable burden for prosecutors, who must establish beyond a reasonable doubt not only that the victim was trafficked but that she was deceived or forced, the restricted definition prevailed. Two years after its passage, only four prosecutions had been brought under the new law.

What is the relation, if any, between prostitution and sex trafficking?

The truth is that what we call sex trafficking is nothing more or less than globalized prostitution. Sex industry profiteers transport girls and women across national and regional borders and "turn them out" into prostitution in locations in which their victims are least able to resist and where there is the greatest demand for them. Ironically, the demand is greatest in countries with organized women's movements, where the status of women is high; and there are relatively few local women available for commercial sexual exploitation. The brothels of the United States, Canada, the Netherlands, Germany, Austria, and Australia are filled with women trafficked from Asia, Latin America, and Eastern Europe. No less than 50 percent of German prostitutes are illegal immigrants and a staggering 80 percent of Dutch prostitutes are not Dutch-born (Owen, 2002; Louis, M., 1999).

Conversely, what most people refer to as "prostitution" is usually domestic trafficking. The bulk of the sex industry involves pimps and other sex industry entrepreneurs controlling women and girls, often by moving them from places in which they have family and friends into locations in which they have no systems of support. Movement is also essential because customers demand novelty. In the United States, for example, there are national and regional sex industry circuits in which prostituted women and girls are rotated among cities, ensuring customers variety and sex-industry entrepreneurs control.

Sex trafficking and prostitution overlap in fundamental ways. Those targeted for commercial sexual exploitation share key characteristics: poverty, youth, and minority status in the country of exploitation, histories of abuse, and little family support. Sex-industry customers exploit trafficked and prostituted women interchangeably for the identical purpose. The sex-industry businesses in which trafficked and prostituted women are exploited are often one and the same, with trafficked and locally prostituted women "working" side-by-side. Local brothels and strip clubs are usually traffickers' destinations and key to their financial success. The injuries that prostituted and trafficked women suffer are identical: post-traumatic stress disorder, severe depression, damage to reproductive systems, damage from sexual assault and beatings, and sexually transmitted diseases.

Certainly international trafficking intensifies the dynamics of power and control that characterize domestic prostitution: the isolation of the victims; their dependence on their abusers; their difficulty in accessing criminal justice and social service systems; and their fear of exposure to the authorities. But the dynamics of trafficking and prostitution are the same dynamics, and their commonalities far overshadow their differences. In spite of efforts to differentiate and separate prostitution and trafficking, the inescapable conclusion is that the difference between the two, at most, is one of degree, not of kind.

If sex trafficking and prostitution were distinct and separate phenomena and if prostitution were as innocuous as trafficking is injurious, a logical response would be to direct criminal sanctions against sex traffickers and legalize and regulate prostitution. This is the position that the Netherlands, Germany, and others following the "Dutch" example have embraced. But the Dutch and German experience–along with those of other jurisdictions that have legalized prostitution–have demonstrated just what happens when prostitution is legitimized and protected by law: the number of sex businesses grows, as does the demand for prostitution. Legalized prostitution brings sex tourists and heightens the demand among local men. Local women constitute an inadequate supply so foreign girls and women are trafficked in to meet the demand. The trafficked women are cheaper, younger, more exciting to customers, and easier to control. More trafficked women means more local demand and more sex tourism. The end result looks a lot like Amsterdam.

The Swedish government, in response to the massive movement of trafficked Eastern European women into its borders, developed an antithetical policy response. In 1999, it passed and implemented legislation that stepped up measures against prostitution, not only by directing strong penalties against pimps, brothel owners, and other sex industry entrepreneurs, but by also directing criminal sanctions against customers. (The law also eliminated penalties against prostitutes, such as the penalty for soliciting.) After the passage of the new law, Sweden spearheaded a public education campaign warning sex industry customers that patronizing prostitutes was criminal behavior. The result was unexpected. While there was not a dramatic decrease in the incidence of prostitution, sex trafficking to Sweden declined while neighboring Scandinavian countries witnessed a significant increase. The danger of prosecution coupled with a diminished demand made Sweden an unpromising market for global sex traffickers.

The antithetical Dutch and Swedish legislative approaches to prostitution and trafficking hold important lessons for social change activists and policy makers. Legalizing and legitimizing domestic prostitution throws out a welcome mat to international sex traffickers. Curtailing the demand for prostitution chills sex trafficking.

Prostitution and sex trafficking are the same human rights catastrophe, whether in local or global guise. Both are part of a system of gender-based domination that makes violence against women and girls profitable to a mind-boggling extreme. Both prey on women and girls made vulnerable by poverty, discrimination, and violence and leaves them traumatized, sick, and impoverished. Both reward predators sexually and financially, strengthening both the demand and criminal operations that ensure the supply. The concerted effort by some NGOs and governments to disconnect trafficking from prostitution–to treat them as distinct and unrelated phenomena–is nothing less than a deliberate political strategy aimed at legitimizing the sex industry and protecting its growth and profitability.

The obvious fact that the demand for prostitution and the demand for trafficked women are one in the same demonstrates the fallacy of this false division. It also reveals our best hope for ending and trafficking and prostitution. As Norma Hotaling has demonstrated in her work to educate and deter buyers and as the Swedish government has shown in arresting buyers, while demand is essential to sex industry success, it also represents the weak link in the sex industry chain. Unlike prostituted women and girls, prostitution customers do have choices to make. And when they see that choosing to buy women devastates lives and threatens their own freedom and social standing, they make different choices. We've seen what works. The domestic violence movement has witnessed a dramatic decline in repeat domestic violence and the incidence of intimate partner homicides following a decades-long program of education, support, and services for victims and, crucially, accountability for abusers through a pro-arrest, pro-prosecution approach. Curtailing the demand for prostitution through accountability for prostitution buyers is the essential next step in our fight to end trafficking and prostitution.

Panel 1:
What Do We Know about the People Who Make Up the "Demand" Side of Sex Trafficking?[1]

Panelist: Stephen Grubman-Black

Deconstructing John

The given task: What do we know about the people who make up the "demand" side of sex trafficking?

I will address my approach to the task by offering ways to identify characteristics of men who use women as sexualized commodities. It is not enough to list or inventory such characteristics. I believe the information is only as important as the degree to which we challenge traditional male role assumptions and begin to deconstruct such a model of behavior and attitudes. Anything short of that is to marginalize, not only the victim, *i.e.*, the women being prostituted, but the victimizer, the men who seek, stalk, use, and abuse women. Men who prostitute women come from the same culture as that which fosters gender inequity and misogyny.

First, I want to state my appreciation for this opportunity and to acknowledge the foresight and dedication of the organizers of this event as well as the activism and other efforts of many who are in attendance.

---

[1] Bracketed comments are summaries provided by Sara Dubin, Amany Ezeldin, and Gil Lenz.

Indirect data. Recently, young adults in two classes I offer at University of Rhode Island: WMS 150 (Introduction to Women's Studies) and WMS 350R (a Special Topics course dealing with sexual victimization) have given me insights that lead me to believe that the depiction of women as objects of desire in pornography is more and more an acceptable factor in the lives of young women and young men. It seems more normal, more acceptable, and the threshold for tolerance is higher and higher. When, for example, I submitted the parameters of degradation and abuse to the equation of what is pornography, arguments still were offered.

Further, they have learned to believe that women in prostitution are in the work because they want to be there. They are either incredulous or shocked by data and evidence that challenges their belief systems. So, being informed about rape and other physical, as well as emotional and financial, abuses against prostitutes was met with some resistance.

As for their views of the men who frequent prostitutes, they are either disgusted or shocked. Men might joke about "having to pay for it," but they feel that by paying for the sexual act, the man is entitled to the woman. But, *they believe that it is the responsibility of the woman to stop.* They are dismayed and sickened by stories of trafficking, but they are ambivalent regarding responsibility. Some (women and men) believe it is based on economics, believing at first that women are paid well for being prostitutes.

I tell them about some of my work. I tell them about some of the men's stories shared with me during interviews. They listen, but I am not sure what they hear and what they learn. At least some of them are moved enough to want to talk more. Most of them are the young women in the classes. Although disgusted, many are ambivalent about responsibility.

My work. What is that demand based upon? The answer is: men's illusions, expectations, and behaviors about themselves regarding sex. Men believe certain fantasies about themselves that influence their interactions with women. When some men approach women, they say, "I'm horny," exaggerate their genitalia size, recall men in their 20s using Viagra, and express "wanting to get off." Many of the men with whom I have interacted (whether through interviews or conversations, during discussions or chats) have a complicated view about the use of women. They demand that a woman be attractive and often equate that

18

attractiveness with availability. They feel, in some sense and to some degree, that their "natural urges" must be met. At the same time, they elevate themselves by presenting themselves as "the best the woman ever had," evidently not seeing the paradox in paying a woman to agree with him about his prowess and endowments. A number of men who frequent prostituted women delude themselves. They seem to belong to a "men's club" that insulates them from caring about the person under them or on her knees before them. Feminists, they are not!

Who are some of the men who discussed their involvement with prostitutes? They represent a mostly Euro-American heterosexual population, between the ages of twenty-two and sixty-five. Many are in some sort of on-going relationship. They believe that what they do, *i.e.*, searching and soliciting a woman for the purposes of sexual activity, is normal and natural for men. Some of them base this belief on earlier experiences, having been initiated into sexual activity with a woman by a visit sponsored by a father, uncle, or other adult male identity figure. It was their first, but lasting, impression of women as second-class citizens.

One man, who represented a cyber resource center "supporting sex work as a badly needed legitimate profession promoting more intimacy, more sensual sexuality," told me that the U.S. needs more adult sexual rights because of the very sad situation here, *i.e.*, that the U.S. lacks creative avenues, but he assured me that "there are many wonderful providers and clients."

So, who are these clients?

[First, Grubman-Black revealed that when he initiated this project (in 1999) to approach men who sought out prostitutes, he put an ad in an alternative newspaper to advertise for men who bought women. Regular newspapers did not want to post advertisements using the word "prostitute." He also put a notice on internet-sites and through word of mouth. Some of the men who responded seemed proud of their prowess and exploits. Grubman-Black communicated with these men through emails, letters, and instant messaging. Through this study, Grubman-Black has created a list of groups of men who make up the demand side of prostitution.]

19

- Lonely, Shy, Awkward

  Men in this grouping believed it was "easier" to pay; they
  wanted to hide their identity. Some of the men in this group
  did not report functional peer relationships with women. One,
  in fact, referred to the prostituted women he paid as "girl
  friends." Another told me that his "regular girlfriend" lived in
  Australia; he saw her once or twice a year. These men did not
  seem interested in having a long-term relationship with a
  woman. It was either too much trouble or, in one example, the
  only way he saw himself having sex (I believe he was a member of a religious order). Sex for them was secretive and
  shameful, yet necessary. One interesting characteristic shared
  among them and between groups actually was a "blame" factor, i.e., women in prostitution "tempt" men even though, during follow-up, the men readily admit to seeking out the
  women.

- Wanting Sexual Activity Not Able to Have with Primary Partner

  The three main reasons given by the men in this sub-group for
  seeking a woman in prostitution were: (1) Oral sex. Men ap-
  peared adamant about their need and right for having fellatio
  performed on them. Further, there was no mutual oral sex
  even considered. It is also significant that they did not use
  condoms, even though they would often insist on ejaculating
  in the woman. (2) Anal sex. Other men liked the feeling of
  anal sex with a woman. My impression was that, similar to
  oral sex, the men could distance themselves from the woman.
  One or two believed this was a good method because pregnancy could be avoided. (3) A threesome (with another man
  with the prostituted woman). Several men reported wanting to
  "experiment." They would watch each other having sex with
  the woman (referring at times to pornography they had
  viewed). Several reported "surprising" the prostituted woman
  and each other by having sex with her and each other at the
  same time.

- Thrill of Adventure, of the Hunt, including Cruising and Surfing

  Men in this group sought excitement. Some of the men spoke of looking for "company" as if they had been on a different type of hunting expedition. Whether behind a wheel or a computer keyboard, they were as sexually excited during the process of finding the woman as they were with her. It was an arousing experience for them. They also desired a feeling of having choice or selection. The cruising and hunting was likened to looking at a menu or looking for a shirt. It was the variety of choice they liked. One or two actually grinned as they recalled the disappointed looks or voices or words they perceived by the ones they did not choose.

- Changing the Rules of Agreement

  These men enjoyed keeping a prostitute beyond the agreed upon time, often by force, *e.g.,* holding her down, locking the door, or staying on top of her, and yet do not perceive this as a violation of her rights. They have no sense of embarrassment about it. The majority of these men agree to use a condom, and then refuse to, offering a defense that they do not want to use one with their "regular" sex partner.

- Roughing Her Up

  [This often is rape, even if the man does not use that term to describe his actions. For example, some men who feel they have been misled get angry and then rough the woman up.] Some of these men became angry because "she" was a "he." The accounts of this occurred during visits to video stores and adult bookstores that offered booths for rent. The three men who reported this told me that they had met on the Internet and arranged to meet inside. During a specific act, usually the preferred "quick fix" of fellatio, they discovered it was a male, "flipped him over," and raped him through forced anal intercourse.

These men did what they did because they could. Based on the expressed disregard for the women, I believe that more men than who reported such behavior had actually raped the woman whose body they believed they "owned." There was an undercurrent of violence in their references to the women, assigning such terms as "whore," "bitch," etc., that suggested to me that misogyny is a theme here. This leads me to recall Ann Salter's term "stinking thinking," referring to her observations among sexual criminals who have hostile attitudes to women; a sense of entitlement; callous indifference to others; and self-serving excuses for their behaviors.

- Taking Directions Via Cameras

  Some men took great care in setting up a room in which they brought a woman and then took directions from other men watching via Internet about what they should "do" to the woman. There was both a sense of performance, as well as vicarious sexual gratification from the act.

- Ultimate Control

  A few of the men liked the power and control of paying a woman for sex. "I pay, I get my way." One of the men reported that he believed that, for the time he had her, he owned her. No holds were barred. He showed no remorse. "I have my say" was a variation of above. This man felt that he could only have "complete freedom" when he bought a woman for sex. "Stay there." One man brought a woman in prostitution to a business meeting. He demanded that she be with him constantly. When she asked him if she could leave to use the toilet facilities, he reported to me that he "denied" her that right. He told her to "stay there."

How and where do males learn to disregard the rights of females?

- Young men's beliefs about women's sexuality based on media and pornography. Many of the young men with whom I interacted (outside the interview part of my research) referred to

22

"recreational pornography." They use these materials (mostly videotapes available from local video stores) for self-stimulation; some introduce the videos to the young women they date who, for the most part, accept this as part of a dating ritual.

- Normalization of sexism and objectification. Many young adult men and women accept the notion that "sex or sexism sells," feeling that it is what most people desire and believe.

- Men's beliefs about their sexuality and urges for gratification. From an early age, many males believe that sexual excitement precedes sexual urges that "should" lead to sexual release. In one sense, many males believe that their genitalia has "a mind of its own." Men who seek women in prostitution want sexual release through the women.

- Normalization of objectification and commoditization. Men and an alarming number of women believe that when a man pays (as on a date), he has certain rights and privileges to her body through sex. Throughout my work, I have found that a "john" is a man who believes he is entitled by virtue of his gender and money to have sex on demand. Whether he is shy or not, whether he calls her a girlfriend or a whore, and whether or not he abides by some set of rules or limits, he believes that he can buy a woman's body for sexual use.

- Lack of discussions of prostitution in men's studies, for example, reflects a serious denial and dismissiveness of taking the issue seriously. A lack of serious challenge within Women's Studies that views prostitution for what it is—namely, enslavement and violence against our sisters—is very troublesome.

I think that we need to reshape the culture–challenge the way a patriarchal culture defines masculinity–addressing fathering, transforming boy culture, and creating men's social activism. So what do I tell a generation of people who still need to learn to believe they live in a rape culture? That prostitution is a violation of women's rights? That men's beliefs, that they are entitled to sex on demand, are not only fallacious, but wrong?

I think what this newer generation needs to know is this: They are part of the population of people who make up the "demand" side of sex trafficking.

Moderator: Kristen Houser

[There is an overlap between the body of work from those working in rape crisis and information known about sex offenders and demand. There is a hierarchy of victimization, and the perceived social status of the victim affects the treatment that the victim receives. There are repercussions when society does not recognize that prostitutes are important. Society needs to criminally prosecute the offenders. The language around prostitution is made up of euphemisms–a market-style vocabulary insisting that prostitution is merely sex work, *i.e.,* the buying and trading of goods. This denial of reality is also similar to the language used by the Catholic Church regarding the abuse by priests. There is a watering down of the word rape to "inappropriate sexual behavior." But it is rape, and these men are sex offenders. We need the voices of survivors in every step of the movement. They have the PhD's in the experience against which we are fighting.]

Panelist: Brenda Myers

[Brenda Myers is a survivor of prostitution. She was a prostitute for 25 years. Currently, she is a single woman, and the only "man" in her life is her cat, Aretha Franklin. She is a grandmother and has recently attained her GED. She has undergone a 12-step prostitution recovery program. She believes that there needs to be more recovery and less incarceration mechanisms available to women in prostitution.

She first remembers being sexually molested when she was four or five years old. The local prostitutes near her home were heroes to her. She decided to be a prostitute when she was nine-years-old because she thought that the value of her body was low. By fifteen, she turned her first trick. The johns taught her what she needed to know more than anyone else. The johns had all the information. Her first trick was a man who asked for a blow job, but she did not know what it was. She blew on the john's penis because she did not know what to do. The john told her what to do. Another man once offered her "a lot of money." She said she wanted $100, and he replied, "Honey, I don't want to buy you, I just want to date you for a while." As she said, "I had a dream of being a 'pretty woman' before the movie ever came out, but I never met Richard Gere and no one ever took me shopping!"

Discussing her life as a prostitute, she suffered countless brutalities: she was shot five times, stabbed thirteen times, and raped countless times. Calling the police is not a viable option for a prostitute, because the police do not acknowledge that a man can rape a prostitute. She has been beaten unconscious many times, as well. She also danced at strip bars at night and worked in massage parlors during the day. As a side note, she talked about how most judges are into S&M, that "they want to get beat."

Then she commented on personal experiences she had with the categories of men who use prostitutes as identified by Grubman-Black:

(1) Lonely and Shy John. She recalled a specific man who was a stalker. He pulled a gun on her and was going to kill her. She said that this group was the most dangerous.

(2) Easy Pay John. Men who want to pay and go. They do not want the responsibility for the act or the feelings. The johns think that once they have paid the money, the act is over and that she deserved what he did to her because he paid her. They had no more responsibility, no matter what they had done because they had paid cash. She also talked about how anyone could be a john.

(3) The Hunter John. These men rode around and watched a prostitute work, even while doing other tricks, before they approached her.

(4) Friendly John. These men do not want you to stop prostituting, but they say they are your "friend." Sometimes they gave her money without asking for a trick. These men were excited to be "friends" with a prostitute.

(5) Rich John. These men would ask her, "What is a nice girl like you doing here?" And she would think to herself, "Well, what is a scumbag like you doing here?"

Myers also talked about instances in which police became involved. The police she encountered never once told the john that he was wrong. The johns never had to show up in court. She would be arrested and the john would be let go. This phenomenon is an example of "guys feeling bad for another guy." She was convicted of a felony. Johns were never judged, and they were never prosecuted even when she had been injured.

Myers reflected on the foundation of her involvement in prostitution. She believed that she was the bad one. Prostituting was more than a way to make money, it reinforced her low perception of her self-worth. She deserved every trick that she turned because she believed that the childhood molestation was her fault. She, therefore, took responsibility for being nothing more than an object of men's sexual desire. She accepted what society told her. Many women do not exit prostitution because they believe it is all they are worth. Her dream was to become a Madame because she had no sense of self-worth that allowed her to imagine doing anything but dealing in prostitution. She said that she always thought she was going to die with a blond wig and a cat suit on.

She emphasized that most of society are johns. They use women as sexual objects because they can, and it is allowed. She does not call prostitution a profession, although people claim it as the oldest profession. She asks, if it is a profession, how would employers advertise for this job? The ads would read: "Do you want to be beaten, abused, raped in every sexual way imaginable? Do you want unemotional sex in the back of an alley, in a car with a baby in the backseat? Do you want to be bought by a father wanting his son to have his first sexual experience with a prostitute as a right of passage?" She has been asked why women remain prostitutes if prostitution is so bad. She answers today, "Because I accepted bad."]

Moderator: Kristen Houser

[People get caught up in academia and policy work, but we need to hear the voices of the survivors.]

Panelist: Melissa Farley

What Do We Know About Johns?

Public awareness about the traumatic harm of prostitution and sex trafficking lags many years behind awareness of the harms of incest, rape, and domestic violence. Yet, the harm is essentially the same. Why is the perpetrator of this harm against the woman, girl, or boy in prostitution socially invisible, and why is the behavior of the john/perpetrator invisible?

In part, prostitution's invisibility is a result of the normalization of prostitution in medicine and in the social sciences. Sexologists Kinsey and Masters & Johnson worked from the 1940s through the 1970s, articulating a prostitution-like sexuality for men and women that was later enthusiastically promoted by Hefner and Hollywood. Today, this presentation of women's sexuality can be seen in popular women's magazines. Experts on women's sexuality are women who are currently prostituting. A 2002 issue of *Marie Claire*, a young women's magazine, contained an article about women's sexuality co-authored by a prostitute in a Nevada brothel and by a woman who had prostituted in more than 50 videos.

Like the public, even women who enter prostitution themselves at first believe these myths about prostitution. Some adolescents have told me that when they entered prostitution, they truly believed that prostitution would be the way it was pictured in *Pretty Woman*: a fun, sexy job where you eventually meet a nice guy. Yet, after leaving prostitution, another woman said that johns were not the "... well-adjusted, merely lonely men, attractive and charismatic, that we had all imagined. They were aggressive, needy, filthy and unwashed." They scammed and tricked her until, disillusioned, she finally left prostitution (Colwell, 2001).

Sexologists, the popular media, and many HIV researchers have removed prostitution from its gender, race, and class context. This facilitates the dissemination of harmful myths about prostitution. Globally, prostitution and sex trafficking victims are overwhelmingly female, overwhelmingly women of color, and overwhelmingly poor. When these facts about prostitution are ignored, prostitution is much more likely to be seen incorrectly as a consenting sex act. There is a massive power imbalance in prostitution, where johns have the social and economic power to hire women, adolescents, girls, or boys to act out their masturbation fantasies (Davidson, 1998, p. 209). The harm she experiences in prostitution is made invisible when it is described not as sexual harassment, not as rape, not as partner violence, but as "sex." The cruelty of prostitution intensifies when it is presented as "something else, when the context has been radically altered, and [its] cruelty is exhibited as something humorous or sexy" (Millett, 1994).

The numbers question

It is impossible to accurately estimate how many men in the world have bought women for sex: They hide. Even where prostitution is legal, most of johns' behaviors are carefully concealed from public view. But we do know that many, many men use prostitutes, especially when we include in our count bachelor parties (called gang-rape parties by women in prostitution), strip clubs where women are prostituted in lap-dancing or "V.I.P. rooms," and live video chats where women are prostituted online.

Johns are average citizens rather than abnormally sadistic psychopaths. They are all ages and from all social classes. Most are married or partnered. Women in prostitution tell us that about half of all johns demand sex acts without a condom. One woman reported that as she was about to perform a blow job in an upscale car, she heard a cry from the back seat, turned around and saw a one-year-old baby strapped into a car seat.

Estimates of the numbers of men who have ever purchased women for sex acts range from 16-80 percent, based on a superficial review of the literature:

Benjamin and Masters (1964)	80%
Thai Public Health Ministry (1990s)[2]	75%
Kinsey (1948)	69%
Monto (1998)	45%
Michael, Gagnon, Laumann & Kolata (1994)	16%.

---

[2]The data from the Thai Public Health Ministry was cited by Bishop & Robinson, 1998, p. 160.

These numbers tell us very little about the prevalence of men's prostituting behaviors. The fact that the percentages seem to be decreasing over time (80 percent in 1964 and 16 percent thirty years later) is likely a fallacious trend that actually reflects an increasing normalization of certain types of prostitution like that occurring in strip clubs or lap-dancing clubs or massage brothels. Escort/internet prostitution enables men to be even more secretive about their prostituting behaviors than was possible twenty years ago (Hughes, 2003).

Research on attitudes toward prostitution

We have begun a series of research studies on attitudes toward prostitution. Rape myths and prostitution myths are components of culturally supported attitudes that normalize violence against women. Prostitution myths justify the existence of prostitution, promote misinformation about prostitution, and contribute to a social climate that exploits and harms not only prostituted women, but all women. Examples of prostitution myths include statements such as: "Women are prostitutes because they want to be, it's their choice;" "The availability of prostitutes makes the rapes of other women less likely;" and "Prostitution should be treated no differently than any other business."

With Ann Cotton, Megan Schmidt, Bob Jensen, Louise Fitzgerald, Linda Collinsworth, Bob Baron, and others, I investigated the relationship between prostitution myth acceptance, rape myth acceptance, and self-reported sexually coercive behaviors. Participants were 783 university undergraduates attending introductory level courses from California, Iowa, Texas, and Oregon. Among our initial findings are:

1) a gender difference in attitudes toward both prostitution and rape, with men more supportive of prostitution and more accepting of rape myths than women;
2) a positive correlation between acceptance of rape myths and support for prostitution;
3) a positive correlation among college men between self-reported sexually coercive behaviors and acceptance of certain specific prostitution myths; and
4) 7 percent of the college students admitted to being johns.

Although they were a statistical minority, the johns were significantly different from the other young men. Those college students who had bought women in prostitution were more accepting of prostitution myths and rape myths than any of the other students. Chillingly, the college-age johns differed from the other students not only in their attitudes, but also in their actual behaviors toward women. They acknowledged having perpetrated more sexually coercive acts with their partners than the other men (Cotton, Farley & Baron, 2002; Cotton, Farley & Schmidt, 2001; Farley, Becker, Cotton, Sawyer, Fitzgerald & Jensen, 1998; Schmidt, Cotton & Farley, 2002).

Prostitution myth acceptance is one of a cluster of harmful attitudes towards women that encourage and justify violence against women. Along with other researchers of violence against women, we think that acceptance of prostitution is connected with other harmful attitudes and abusive behavior toward women. Violent behaviors against women have been associated with attitudes that promote men's beliefs that they are entitled to sexual access to women, that they are superior to women, and that they are licensed as sexual aggressors (White & Koss, 1993). Johns strongly endorse these attitudes toward women. If we are serious about preventing prostitution and other violence against women, we need to address the development of men's attitudes toward women when they are pre-adolescent, much younger than college-age.

Here is what johns tell us about prostitution:

"If your wife stops having sex with you, what choices do you have? You can beat the hell out of her, like a lot of guys do, or, if you're someone like me who works six days a week and doesn't go to the health club and isn't going to find a girlfriend, you can go to a hooker." (Dobie, 2000, p.174).

"It's like going to have your car done, you tell them what you want done, they don't ask, you tell them you want so and so done..." (McKeganey & Barnard, 1996, p. 53).

"I use them like I might use any other amenity, a restaurant or a public convenience. It answers my needs. No questions, no answers, no future. It's clean, it's efficient, it's over. I've never made the mistake of falling for them" (Seabrook, 1996, p. 193).

"I've thought a lot about this, and asked a lot of people about this, and it comes down to 'I wanted a piece of ass and she was there'" (Benjamin & Masters, 1964, p. 196).

Viewing himself as an international humanitarian, one U.S. john in Thailand stated: "These girls gotta eat, don't they? I'm putting bread on their plate. I'm making a contribution. They'd starve to death unless they whored" (Christopher Moore, cited in Bishop & Robinson, 1998, p. 168).

An Indian john said, "When there is violence, it is mostly the prostitute's fault. See, I am going to buy something. If I am satisfied with what I am buying, then why should I be violent? I will be violent when I am cheated, when I am offered a sub-standard service... Sometimes violence is because the prostitute wants the client to use condoms. They force it on the client. He will naturally be disgruntled and there will be altercations" (Anderson & Davidson, 2003, p 24).

It's time to turn the spotlight on the john. With thanks to Paula Caplan's writings and Michelle Anderson's consultation, here is a new psychiatric diagnosis:

Predatory Erectile Disorder (PRED)[3]

1. **PREDs** have an inability to establish and maintain meaningful relationships with women.[4]

---

[3]Michelle Anderson and Nikki Craft contributed to the name of the johns' "psychiatric disorder": Predatory Erectile Disorder or PRED.

[4]Paula Caplan responded to the American Psychiatric Association's proposal to list a women's psychiatric disorder: Masochistic Self-Defeating Personality Disorder - with her own Delusional Dominating Personality Disorder. She brilliantly critiqued the sexism in the Diagnostic and Statistical Manual of Mental Disorders , the diagnostic sourcebook widely used by mental health professionals in the United States. Items 1, 2 , and 4 are verbatim items from Caplan's Delusional Dominating Personality Disorder, also typical of johns with Predatory Erectile Disorder. Item 5 is verbatim from Caplan, except for the word "commercial" which was supplied by Michelle Anderson.

2. **PREDs** are unable to identify and express a range of feelings in themselves (typically accompanied by an inability to identify accurately the feelings of other people).

3. **PREDs** chronically equate sex with dominance rather than mutuality.

4. **PREDs** tend to use verbal and physical coercion rather than negotiation in the face of interpersonal conflict.

5. **PREDs** need to affirm their social importance by displaying themselves in the company of females who meet any three of the following criteria:

    a. are commercially physically attractive

    b. are younger than themselves

    c. are shorter in stature than themselves

    d. weigh less than themselves

    e. appear to be lower on socioeconomic criteria than themselves

    f. are more submissive than themselves

6. **PREDs** should be screened for a life history that has trained them to justify abuse of or contempt toward women. **PREDs** are exposed at an early age to pornography in which there was repeated reinforcement for the treatment of women as prostitutes (*i.e.*, treating women as sub-human or not-human) by their fathers, brothers, friends, or the media.

7. **PREDs** seek either to purchase women in prostitution or to treat women as prostitutes in any and all venues including strip clubs, universities, massage parlors, courtrooms, social gatherings, the street, the supermarket, conferences, and elsewhere.

What else do we know about johns?

The myth of emotional mutuality

    Against the evidence and against common sense, johns insist that prostitutes truly enjoy the rape-like sex of prostitution. Johns are committed to the fiction that prostitution is an equal exchange: sex acts for money. Yet, there is a major contradiction for the john. While he knows that his money and his purchase of her gives him the control while it removes her autonomy and her dignity–despite this inequality, he hopes that she really likes him and is sexually aroused by him. Plumridge (1997) points out that on the one hand, johns believed that commercial sex was a mutually pleasurable exchange, and, on the other hand, they believed that payment of money removed all social and ethical obligations. Since she's getting paid for acting as if she really likes him and as if she is sexually aroused by him-she performs. The john usually has to fool himself into believing that she is a "whore with a heart of gold" who cares about him, or that "she's a young, naïve girl who's never been fucked by a real man before," or that "she secretly loves putting her high heel on his testicles while whipping him." He usually attempts to get more than he's paying for; that's why he's called a "trick." Johns trick women by inflicting more sexual assaults for the money than the women are paid for.

Men who buy women in prostitution deny that they harm women. "Dave" (2003), for example, lists several articles on his website describing the medical benefits of breast massage. He then states that because he massages the breasts of the women he buys in prostitution, he is thereby promoting women's health.

Prostitution is about the hunt

Discussing his experience of being in a strip-club, one man said "This is the part of me that can still go hunting" (Frank 1999). I was surprised when several johns told me that they did not particularly enjoy sex with women in prostitution. If prostitution wasn't for the sex, I wondered, what was it about? Their answer was: *It's the hunt*. The johns savored and were sexually excited by the challenge of finding the location where "bad" women could be found, stalking her, hiding their motivations from passers-by (so they thought), negotiating a price, and eventually "scoring the kill," *i.e.*, winning the game by buying and paying for the rape.

With the online name of "hunter," another john posted reports of "missions" on which he hunts down and scores "hits" of women in prostitution.[5] Advertising a "sex safari," South African pimp/rancher Johan Maree hired women in prostitution to be hunted down with paintball guns by johns who would then have sex with them.[6] Similar

---

[5] http://www.milfhunter.com/main.htm?id=jt6838&p=clean&t=no

[6] See: Philp, R. (1999) Boerewors goes cold as sex hunt flops. South Africa Sun-Times. August 8, 1999. Retrieved from: http://www.suntimes.co.za/1999/08/08/news/news20.htm See also: Dispatch Online (1999) Bikers' Hunt for Prostitutes Peters Out. South Africa Dispatch Online August 9, 1999. Retrieved from: http://www.dispatch.co.za/1999/08/09/southafrica/PROS.HTM

events have been orchestrated in the United States. The Society for the Prevention of Cruelty to Animals in South Africa complained that the wildlife on the game farm would be traumatized by the event.[7]

Prostitution is training for and the practice of dominance over women
A woman who worked in Japanese men's clubs learned to perform a ritualized subservience. Whether he talks about his thirty-foot penis or his stamp collection, in her role as hostess, the woman must proclaim that the qualities he has revealed are exactly what a woman like herself finds irresistibly attractive (Allison, 1994).

Shows of ritualized sexual dominance are as much for the benefit of other men as they are for the woman who is stripping or prostituting. Many men are first encouraged to buy prostitutes by other men. Whether it is a group outing to a strip club, a first visit to a brothel, or a bachelor party, a performance is expected of the john: he is taught to ogle, yell at her, and sexually harass her verbally and physically. In these settings, ritualistic sexual exploitation occurs where men learn to distance themselves from their own feelings, to shut out awareness of the humanity of the woman in prostitution, to dominate her in a way that competes with other men, and to treat her like an object. He is learning how to treat all women.

Prostitution and trafficking are constructed out of the multitude of ways that men hurt women. The "nice guy" mask aside, an unmistakable substrate of intense hatred for women exists in johns. The sex, race, and class inequality of prostitution, with john on top and the woman on the bottom, directly harms her (Farley et al., 2003). In addition, this inequality creates the context for ongoing harm to other women in his life–his wife and daughters and female employees, for example. The interactions between john and prostitute can thus be seen as practice in dehumanizing women. For the john, prostitution is a training ground where he learns a myriad of techniques to subordinate women (Margaret Baldwin, personal communication, October 16, 2003). Often using pornography as his training manual, he tries out a variety of dehumanizing tactics on prostitutes.

Among these brutal dehumanizing tactics is the verbal abuse inflicted by the john on the woman he is prostituting. Although there is a developing recognition of the physical violence in prostitution–the

---

[7] See Philp, R. (1999) Wild Game Hunt for Sex South Africa Sun-Times. August 1, 1999. Retrieved from: http://www.suntimes.co.za/1999/08/01/news/news18.htm

rapes, the beatings, the physical intimidation–we have yet to adequately comprehend the overwhelming verbal cruelty perpetrated by the john against the woman in prostitution. The acts perpetrated against her cause not only physical harm; they verbally and psychologically define her as object, as degraded, as "cunt," as "filthy whore." Her self, her individuality, her humanness is systematically attacked and destroyed in prostitution. The john reduces her to vagina, anus, breasts, and mouth. She ultimately acts the part of the thing men want her to be, and, in the process, she may eventually believe those things about herself (Dworkin, 1997).

Normalized in most cultures, prostitution is nonetheless what might well be described as a "harmful traditional cultural practice," a term applied internationally to female genital mutilation that refers to customs that are "based on the idea of the inferiority or the superiority of either of the sexes or on stereotyped roles for men and women." The behavior of johns should be seen in this context (MacKinnon, 2001; Wynter, Thompson & Jeffreys, 2002).[8]

The Swedish Minister for Gender Equality, Margareta Winberg, announced a campaign in 2001 to address the harm of prostitution at the source. The slogan of Sweden's campaign was "No customers, no prostitution." I thank the organizers of this conference for bringing us together to focus on johns. Prostitution and trafficking cannot be eliminated without the understanding that johns are socially tolerated predators of women.

---

[8] A United Nations General Assembly resolution (A/RES/54/133, 7 Feb. 2000) addressed the harm of female genital mutilation using language from the Convention on the Elimination of All Forms of Discrimination Against Women (CEDAW). The resolution requires states' parties to take all appropriate measures "to modify the social and cultural patterns of conduct of men and women, with a view to achieving the elimination of prejudices and customary and all other practices which are based on the idea of the inferiority or the superiority of either of the sexes or on stereotyped roles for men and women." For further information on these concepts see C.A. MacKinnon (2001) *Sex Equality*, pgs. 1590-91.

References

Anderson, B. & Davidson, J.O. (2003) *Is Trafficking in Human Beings Demand Driven? A Multi-Country Pilot Study.* Geneva: International Organization for Migration.

Benjamin, Harry B. and Masters, R.E.L. (1964) Prostitution and Morality: a definitive report on the prostitute in contemporary society and analysis of the causes and effects of the suppression of prostitution. New York: Julian Press.

Bishop, R. and Robinson, L. S. (1998) Night Market: Sexual Cultures and the Thai Economic Miracle. New York: Routledge.

Caplan, P. J. (1995) "They say you're crazy: how the world's most powerful psychiatrists decide who's normal." Reading, MA: Addison-Wesley.

Colwell, D. (2001) "Confessions of a Call Girl's Friend." http://www.alternet.org/story.html?StoryID=11836. October 31, 2001.

Cotton, A., Farley, M., & Baron, R. (2002) "Attitudes toward Prostitution and Acceptance of Rape Myths." Journal of Applied Social Psychology 32 (9): 1790-6.

Cotton, A., Farley, M., and Schmidt, M. (2001) "Prostitution Myth Acceptance, Sexual Violence, and Pornography Use." Presentation at Annual Meeting of the American Psychological Association, San Francisco CA. August 27, 2001.

Crowell, N.A. and Burgess, A.W. (eds.) (1996). Understanding Violence Against Women. Washington, D.C.: National Academy Press.

Dave (2003) Accessed July 2003: http://www.sexworktoronto.com/massage/breastmassage.html

Davidson, J.O. (1998) Prostitution, Power, and Freedom. Ann Arbor: University of Michigan Press.

Dobie, K. (2000) Dear John. VIBE June/July 2000. 171-6.

Dworkin, A. (1997). "Prostitution and Male Supremacy" in Life and Death. New York: Free Press.

Farley, M., Becker, T., Cotton, A., Sawyer, S., Fitzgerald, L., Jensen, R. (1998) "The Attitudes toward Prostitution Scale: College Students' Responses Compared to Responses of Arrested Johns." 14th Annual Meeting of the International Society for Traumatic Stress Studies, Washington, D.C. November 21, 1998.

Farley, M., Cotton, A., Lynne, J., Zumbeck, S., Spiwak, F., Reyes, M.E., Alvarez, D., Sezgin, U. (2003) "Prostitution & Trafficking in Nine Countries: An Update on Violence and Posttraumatic Stress Disorder." Prostitution, Trafficking and Traumatic Stress, M. Farley (ed.) (2003) Binghamton, NY: Haworth.

Frank, K. (1999) Intimate Labors: Masculinity, Consumption, and Authenticity in Five Gentlemen's Clubs. Unpublished doctoral dissertation, Duke University, Durham, N.C.

Hughes, D. (2003) "Prostitution Online." Prostitution, Trafficking and Traumatic Stress.c M. Farley (ed.) (2003) Binghamton, NY: Haworth.

Kinsey, A.C., Pomeroy, W.B., & Martin, C.E. (1949). Sexual Behavior in the Human Male. Philadelphia, W.B. Saunders.

MacKinnon, C.A. (2001) Sex Equality. New York: Foundation Press.

Masters, W. & Johnson, V. (1973). "Ten Sex Myths Exploded." The Sensuous Society. Chicago: Playboy Press.

Michael, RT; Gagnon, JH, Laumann, E.O. and Kolata, G (1994) Sex in America: A Definitive Survey. Boston: Little, Brown & Co.

Millett, Kate (1994) The Politics of Cruelty: an essay on the literature on political imprisonment. New York: WW Norton.

Monto, M. (1998). "Holding Men Accountable for Prostitution: The Unique Approach of the Sexual Exploitation Education Project (SEEP)." Violence Against Women 4: 505-17.

Plumridge,E.W., Chetwynd, J.W., Reed, A., & Gifford, S.J. (1997) "Discourses of Emotionality in Commercial Sex: The Missing Client Voice." Feminism & Psychology 7: 165-181.

Schmidt, M., Cotton, A.& Farley, M. (2000) "Attitudes toward prostitution and self-reported sexual violence." Presentation at the 16th Annual Meeting of the International Society for Traumatic Stress Studies, San Antonio, Texas, November 18, 2000.

White, J.W. & Koss, M.P. (1993) "Adolescent Sexual Aggression within Heterosexual Relationships: Prevalence, Characteristics, and Causes." The Juvenile Sex Offender, Barbaree, H.E., Marshall, W.L. & Laws, D.R. (eds.) New York: Guilford Press.

Wynter, B., Thompson, D. & Jeffreys, S. (2002) "The UN Approach to Harmful Traditional Practices." International Feminist Journal of Politics 4: 72-94.

Panel 1: Questions and Answers

[Question: (Steven Wagner) Is the absence of a positive relationship with a male role model in the formative years a reason why some men are johns?

Answer: (Mary Ann Layden) Most johns are not coming to her for psychotherapy, rather they are depressed. "Childhood abuse is the royal road to adulthood pathology." Many johns come from a background of child abuse. So, yes, a healthy relationship with the father is important for men and women. But a close relationship with a father can be "toxic." A close fatherly bond can be harmful when the father sends sexist messages.

Question: (Stephen Wagner) Is a healthy relationship with the father an inoculation factor against becoming a john or an abusive adult?

Answer: (Mary Ann Layden) If the relationship is healthy, it can help. However, the bond itself will not protect from john behavior unless the father sends positive messages.

Question: (Derek Ellerman) Is creating an addiction to pornography a way out, a way to validate John behaviors? How do you deal with these criticisms?

Answer: (Mary Ann Layden) Psychopathology is not an excuse. Unless the person is seriously mentally ill, they are still responsible for their behaviors. Once pathological gambling came to be seen as an addiction, it became possible that one could be addicted to something that was not an addictive substance. Recognizing the addictiveness of pornography helps to explain behavior that exploits and harms women. If acting out inappropriately, these people should get help. Even if we developed a diagnostic category for pornography, this diagnosis would not be an excuse for harmful behavior. Even if someone would claim that this sexual expression is normal, a response would be that we do a lot of unnatural things for the good of society. It is not in our genes to seek out prostitutes. There are no genes that predispose us for arousal to a garter belt. No one gets a pass because he or she is psychologically disturbed. Some perpetrators say that if they try to control their sexuality, something that [to them] is natural, they will go berserk. We know that controlling something "natural" does not make us crazy.

Comment: (Kristin Houser) Society holds alcoholics accountable if they kill people while driving drunk, so it should hold others accountable for their actions as well.

Question: (unidentified speaker) Does prostitution and pornography trigger obsessive/compulsive behavior?

Answer: (Brenda Myers) Yes, because every sexual predator I have seen has been "obsessed." There is a small group of johns who are obsessive/compulsive, but they are acting out because there are no consequences for their behavior. Their behavior is living up to the idea about doing something without getting punished because society says that harmful behavior to women is permissible. Society has said that a man can even kill a prostitute without any consequences. Myers herself felt that she was obsessive/compulsive about prostitution. She had to go through a 12-step program to get away from the obsessive/compulsive behavior. Johns feel like there is no risk for them and finding a prostitute is part of the hunt. The john mindset is: there are no risks, I am in control, and I can do what I want. If johns could skin prostitutes and put them on their wall as trophies of their conquests, they would. Prostitutes are just something to conquer.

Comment: (unidentified speaker): Patrick Karns, leader of sexual addiction genre, wrote that prostitution is an addiction where these is no victim. In my program for prostitution, men say that the U.S. just doesn't have it right, but Amsterdam has it right. However, the legalized, controlled systems are recruiting areas for Johns. People go to Amsterdam and see the women and it is depressing. Young men and around getting the women, turning them down, and saying things like: "Your tits aren't big enough," "I wouldn't buy you." We need to confront men with the myths that they believe and their harmful consequences to women, society, and the men themselves. No one tells the johns about the lies, that the prostitutes do not really like being a prostitute. It is like the Marlboro man getting on the horse, yet everyone denying that nicotine is addicting. It is deadly, but these men see what they are supposed to do to be considered manly.

Comment: (Stephen Grubman-Black) We need to give the message to men that demand causes real damage to themselves and others. For example, the money they spend on prostitutes could go to help their own families. Also, we have to hit men where it hurts to get them to curb their behavior.

Comment: (Mary Ann Layden) Telling men that a higher proportion of men that look at pornography have premature ejaculation may deter them from partaking in an act that can lead to greater degradation. If you tell them that their sexual function will be disrupted, then they care. If there is more research that it is damaging to sexual performance, then maybe it will help.

Question: (Meg Baldwin) I represent prostituted women who have been sentenced for homicide and who are seeking relief or clemency. Many people do not believe the levels of violence and abusiveness that are part of the interactions with prostitution. We somehow believe that the interactions with a prostitute are just as johns describe it. All we hear from johns is that sex with a prostitute is a consumable experience and, therefore, is void of any relationship between him and the woman. If he seeks out the interaction because it is distant, then we believe that the relationship is actually distant, and thus not as bad. It sounds as if no actual relationship is going on and society believes that his description actually describes the act. I once asked an author of a book about pornography the following questions: if an objectified woman is all that certain men desire, why do they have to use real women? Why can=t men just look at pictures? Are the underlying currents of objectifying women the same in pornography as in prostitution? The author=s response was that men want to be with living objectified women because there is power involved in an interaction with a woman. We cannot truly imagine the interaction between a john and a prostitute if we believe the interaction is distant and cold. If prostitution is just about depersonalized sex, why do the interactions turn emotional, abusive, and dirty? Men perform aggressive displays of filth. Johns can come dirty because the prostitute is lower than he is. This power differential breeds abuse.

Comment: (Brenda Myers) A john believes, "I can come how I want to come because I am paying her." Also, violence can be born when a john cannot perform. He comes to a prostitute because he needs her "professional" help. He comes to her frustrated, and if he continues to not to perform, he blames the prostitute; that is when violence happens. This is when some women kill the johns. There are very volatile emotions. Prostitution is not just depersonalized sex. Men come to heal emotional wounds and improve their self-esteem.

Comment: (Stephen Grubman-Black) Some men that use prostitutes are misogynistic. They will use and abuse women, especially prostitutes.

Comment: (Mary Ann Layden) Some johns have low self-esteem and want to make themselves feel better. Being with a prostitute increases their sense of self-esteem because they believe that they are better than she is.

Comment: (Melissa Farley) Even in places such as Zambia, where there was a 90 percent unemployment rate, men never became prostitutes. Women became prostitutes and men sold pencils.

Comment: (Susan Breault) There are marketing and entrepreneurial tactics underlying the sex industry. This plays into the idea that men cruise around for two hours before they choose a prostitute. Pimps place women under commercial signs advertising a "big sale."

Question: (Sandra Hunnicutt) Is Europe doing better or worse than the U.S. in regards to this problem?

Answer: (Mary Ann Layden) Europe lags behind the United States.[9]

---

[9] See Panel 3 for discussions about how other countries respond to these issues.

41

Question: (Sara Dubin) If all men are exposed to similar influences, such as the media and a patriarchal society, why do some men not go to prostitutes?

Answer: (Brenda Myers) Somewhere along the way, those guys got it, that women are not meat and they are not second class citizens. Until the media and police put as much pressure on johns to stop their behavior as they do on the prostitutes, the trade will continue. The trafficking will continue because as certain women are prohibited from remaining in a city, new women will take their place. The supply travels to the demand, but the demand is always present. A minimum wage job will turn a woman back to prostitution and the felony charges for a prostitute greatly decreases the chance that a prostitute will be able to change her life after she has been released from jail. If the prostitute was homeless when she was arrested, now she really has nowhere to go. The first thing she must do when she gets out of jail is turn a trick in order to eat and find a place to stay. The police are charging the women with felonies, while they pat the johns on the back. The most the police officers do is tow the john=s car, "but their cars didn=t date me!"

Question: (Erin Abrams) What characteristics are apparent in men who go abroad for foreign prostitutes or look for women of different races?

Answer: (Brenda Myers) They want every "flavor of the rainbow."

Answer: (Kristin Houser) Many men create scripts for their perfect scenario. They will invest time and money to go abroad for sex tourism to make their fantasies a reality.

Answer: (unidentified speaker) Some men return to where they served in the armed forces. Foreign troops stationed in those countries establish future epidemic exploitation of that population. These communities are economically vulnerable.

Question: (Tommy Calvert) What should advocates do to reach out to prostitutes to work together to combat prostitution? How can we reach out to those that do not yet see the overlap between sex slavery and prostitution?

Answer: (Brenda Myers) Members of my group of survivors of prostitution are putting together a manual of the dos and don=ts when working with prostitutes. The most important guideline is not to judge. Do not assume that you know her story. If you listen to what she tells you, you could help save her life. If you do not judge her, she might give herself a chance.

Answer: (Kristin Houser) Communities could set up a court watch in order to see who is getting arrested for prostitution. They can keep track of the charges, who was convicted, and the severity of the penalties. Many court-watch groups have found that the johns are falling through the cracks.

Answer: (Brenda Myers) Johns must be held accountable. Courts should fine them and use the money to help the women in prostitution recover.

Question: (unidentified speaker) How can we roll back entitlement? If men go to prostitutes because they feel entitled to, how can we combat this?

Answer: (Mary Ann Layden) Challenge the belief that says they are entitled. She sat outside of a strip club and handed out pamphlets on psychotherapy for people with sex addictions. The group also chanted, AOnly losers pay!" These men did not come back to that club because they did not expect to be challenged. Judges also need to do more, for example, give out fines and jail time, etc.

Answer: (Melissa Farley) We should redefine the discussion. We must translate the sense of entitlement. We must make it critical that women in prostitution are entitled to safety, housing, and medical care. Also, we must articulate that prostitution is battery, not a job. Most people do not know that sexual abuse as a child is almost a prerequisite for becoming a prostitute. We must frame prostitution as paid rape.

Answer: (Brenda Myers) When police are arresting a prostitute they are also locking up a mother. They are arresting and jailing women whose children must now be put in foster care. These restrictions must be applied to men also. The courts must lock up men for felonies, not just the prostitutes.

Question: (Marsha Liss) We must rethink men's behavior. It is not enough to deal with the problems after they have occurred. We need to prevent men from going down the path all together. Only then can we eradicate this behavior. When men get to college, they have already been programmed. When should we start educating men about sexual exploitation and what they can do about it?

Answer: (Mary Ann Layden) Begin at eight years old. Nine is a critical year. Even with education, peer pressure can override it.

Answer: (Brenda Myers) She began thinking about sex at nine years old when she became aware of prostitutes. Now she gets called to talk at schools because seventh graders are having sex in school.

Answer: (Stephen Grubman-Black) We have to start early, young. Resistance is not a reason to ignore the problem. There was a program created in Rhode Island for children, but a number of schools refused the programs. We need to talk about how males are socialized to treat females.

Comment: (Kristen Houser) Through the Violence Against Women Act, Congress has allotted $80 million to the Rape Prevention Education Fund. This money is dedicated to rape prevention programs, not rape services. Congress has only appropriated $40 million of the fund. This money can be used to teach different social norms. Education programs can teach children to look at their lives differently.

Comment: (Twiss Butler) Both boys and girls suffer from bullying in school. Bullying can later be manifested as pimp abuse or dating abuse. Title IX requires a civil society in schools. We must make the connection between bullying and sexual exploitation in school programs that confront bullying.

Question: (Marissa Ugarte) The major problem with funding is that there are so many mixed messages about legalization, decriminalization, and prostitution as work. The government could get confused and fund the wrong people. How can we make our message clear?

Answer: (Brenda Myers) Prostitution should not be legalized. Legal prostitution is like prison or slavery because the women are not allowed to leave the houses. Legalization will only be a shield for slavery. Many women will never be able to get help because prostitution will hide behind the law. The Prostitution Alternative Roundtable (PART) discusses these issues. It costs $14,000 per year to help a prostitute recover but it costs $26,000 per year to keep her incarcerated.

Question: (Donna Hughes) Are pro-prostitution groups getting in the way of programs to help women exit prostitution?

Answer: (Brenda Myers) The resistance mainly comes from the community. Many people see prostitution as a police issue, not as a community issue. They believe the best way to stop prostitution in their neighborhoods is to lock up the prostitutes. Often, when a prostitute is released from jail, she will most likely return to the same community because it is familiar. The cycle continues because now she needs the money more than she did before she was arrested.

Answer: (Mary Ann Layden) Legalization of prostitution leads to an increased number of johns because legalization fosters permission-giving beliefs.

Comment: (Melissa Farley) We have an obligation to take the legalization issue head on. We must speak out against the institution and refute and rebut each of their claims.]

Panel 2:
How Do Consumers of Sex Trafficking Find Their "Supply" and How Is Demand Manipulated and Maintained?[1]

Moderator: Laura Lederer[2]

Panelist: Derek Ellerman

[Mr. Ellerman emphasized that demand is the real cause of trafficking. The solutions and preventative measures for trafficking must, therefore, aim to combat the demand. In this presentation, Mr. Ellerman addressed how buyers find their supply and how this knowledge can be used to aid in victim identification. Polaris Project is a grassroots non-profit organization based in Washington, D.C., working on sex trafficking issues with local, national, and international programs. Polaris Project conducts community-based investigations in partnership with police, conducts direct victim outreach to brothels, and operates three 24-hour hotlines. The organization also oversees the National Trafficking Alert System (NTAS), which focuses on finding cases of trafficking that remain unidentified by law enforcement. Polaris Project's dedicated research site can be found at www.humantrafficking.com.

---

[1] Bracketed comments are summaries provided by Sara Dubin, Shelly Geppert, and Christine Shepard.

[2] Did not submit remarks for publication.

47

There is a crisis in the United States right now; there are around tens of thousands of sex trafficking victims in the U.S. Congress passed a trafficking law in 2000, the Victims of Trafficking and Violence Protection Act of 2000. If utilized, the law would provide services to survivors of trafficking. Much of the money is not being used, however, because the victims are not being identified. Law enforcement does not have the resources to do federal investigation on trafficking cases. The local officials are not trained and do not feel empowered to act because there are no laws such as the Trafficking Act of 2000 at the state level. Community-based groups, therefore, need to take the lead. The trafficking networks are good at what they do and will always be better funded than criminal justice. Polaris Project recognizes that in order to find the victims of trafficking, it must use the strengths of the trafficking networks against the networks themselves.

By understanding how johns find their supply, the Polaris Project is able to do the initial proactive identification of the consumers and then it can bring law enforcement directly to the root of trafficking–the demand. Word of mouth, advertising, and the Internet are the three main ways that the demand finds the supply. Word of mouth involves person-to-person advertising, especially in smaller communities where neighborhood brothels are prevalent. Person to person advertising is the dominant method used in closed brothel systems. In a closed brothel system, the traffickers, the buyers, and the women are of the same community. A common mode of advertising is on business cards that provide the address of the brothel, while falsely promoting a different business. This system has been an effective way to keep law enforcement out because cards are only given to chosen people in the community. Polaris Project trains Latino and Asian male volunteers to go to the communities and locate the brothels. The Polaris Project then conveys vital information to law enforcement if sex trafficking is present.

Advertising is another method to connect the demand with the supply. Most of the advertising is printed in mainstream media outlets. For example, the *Washington Post* publishes advertisements for brothels promoting the sexual services of girls as young as thirteen and fourteen. Newspapers collect an estimated $1.5 million per year from such advertisements. The complicity of corporations, such as newspaper publishers, is vital to the success of these decentralized criminal networks. Advertising is even used in closed brothel systems in non-English newspapers.

The Internet is the virtual equivalent of word of mouth. Through advertisements, websites, and message boards, Internet use is a cost-cutter for traffickers because buyers advertise themselves. There are sites for both buyers and johns in which particular areas, prostituted women, law enforcement patterns, and cities relative to the supply of and access to sex are rated. The Internet is the main tool used to promote sex tourism. For example, the World Sex Guide, a website, is dedicated to providing a forum for the free and open exchange of information regarding prostitution throughout the world. The sites explain in explicit detail the destinations of johns, the location of brothels, and the operational details of such networks. This information, however, aids victim outreach efforts by directing organizations like the Polaris Project to the sources of trafficking.

Demand is maintained mostly through cultural attitudes. These attitudes provide a rationalization for buyers to abuse women and children. Because johns often know what they are doing is wrong, they label the women as sluts and whores, therefore implying that the women deserve their degrading treatment. The men also rationalize their behavior by thinking that they are empowering the women through their monetary support. The disregard for the human dignity of women and the cultural sense of male entitlement to women's bodies maintain the demand for prostitutes by reinforcing the tolerance and complicity of law enforcement. In addition, the media reifies the objectification of women through pornographic images that help to maintain violent attitudes. The Polaris Project is using the same information that traffickers and johns use to locate prostitutes in order to protect the women and children enslaved in sexual bondage.]

Panelist: Jackson Katz

[Mr. Jackson Katz focused on the use of language in several key respects. He argued that we need a conceptual or paradigm shift in our thinking about gender violence: "violence against women" must no longer be seen as only a "women's issue" that some men get involved in, but rather as a men's and women's issue. For example, he said, calling rape a "women's issue" obscures the fact that whether the victims are female or male, men perpetrate ninety-nine per cent of rapes. If men commit over ninety-nine per cent of rape, why do we call it a women's issue?

The roots of imbalance reside in patriarchal constructions of masculinity, which is reified through the common usage of the passive voice to describe acts of violence "against women." Katz shared some insights about the power of the passive voice from the work of Julia Penelope, a feminist linguist.

Consider the following series of sentences:

John beat Mary (active voice). "John" is the subject. "Beat" is the verb. "Mary" is the object. The emphasis of the speech is on what John did to Mary.

Mary was beaten by John (passive voice). "Mary" is the subject. "Was beaten" is the verb. The emphasis of the speech is on the victim.

Mary was beaten.

Mary was battered.

Mary is a battered woman.

The political effect of the passive voice is that John, the batterer, is removed from our consciousness and absolved of responsibility. It's now Mary's problem–she's a "battered woman." At the end of the set of sentences, no one is held accountable and it becomes much easier to blame the victim (Mary). Katz acknowledged that sometimes it is necessary to use the passive voice, especially when the speaker/writer is a woman who needs to avoid antagonizing men (or women) with straightforward language that holds men accountable. But, he argued, when we use the passive voice we should be intentional about it and not simply do it unconsciously.

Katz adapted the Julia Penelope exercise on battering and passive voice to a discussion about prostitution

Consider the political effect of language in the context of prostitution:

John forced Mary into prostitution (active voice).

Mary was forced into prostitution by John (passive voice).

Mary was forced into prostitution.

Mary was a prostituted woman.

Mary is a prostitute.

The passive voice is a common way we describe situations of "violence against women," which underlines willful male ignorance about the reality of men's violence against women. A conservative estimate is that 56 percent of American men have paid prostitutes for sex. Think about the friends and family members of these men. Are they complicit? The linguistic focus on the victim also provides a means for men–and women–to deny what a brother, husband, father, son, or friend is doing to other women.

Since American culture has been conditioned to focus on the victim and ignore the perpetrator, we legitimize men's violent behavior against women. For example in California's gubernatorial election, incredibly no one mentioned candidate Larry Flynt's misogyny. Yet, among other things, he runs a pornography website called "Barely Legal," in which young women sexually pose as even younger girls. Katz read a letter from Ron Oliver to the editor of the LA Times expressing his disappointment that Flynt was not elected. Oliver referred to Flynt as a successful man running a "legitimate business"–never mentioning that it is a business that exploits women and objectifies children as sexual objects of desire.

Feminists who are pro-prostitution contribute to a cultural mentality that excuses the damage men cause to women when they purchase their bodies for sex. This endorsement of prostitution by (some) women is a powerful rationale for men who use it to justify their support for prostitution (or patronage) because it's a woman's "choice."

In addition to avoiding accountability linguistically, which is often part of an unconscious process, certain aspects of male peer culture normalize men's degrading treatment of women. There are many dynamics in male peer culture that define what is expected of men in order to be considered "real men." Bachelor and fraternity parties, military initiations, and all-male work environments where men go to strip clubs together after work are examples of how men define acceptable (and expected) male behavior. Many men, however, are unhappy about the actions and mentalities of their peers. Although many men may want to leave the fraternity party or not go to the strip club, they are bullied and pressured into silence. Many men will continue to compromise their beliefs about the degrading treatment of women out of fear of standing against their fellow males. Male leadership is necessary in order to speak against the dominant culture's insistence that men are entitled to patronize women. Older men, mentors, celebrities, and athletes who occupy leadership platforms should say that men must treat women with dignity and respect. The development over the past few years of anti-sexist men's groups in the U.S. and internationally are promising steps.]

Panelist: Marisa Ugarte

[Ms. Ugarte discussed the invasion of Latin America by those who traffick women and children into all areas of the sex industry. She provided an outline of her remarks that summarizes her main points.]

Latin America has been a forgotten land regarding issues of exploitation and trafficking. Poverty, religious concepts, corruption in the government, and civil unrest make life almost unbearable for the marginalized population of these countries. This has resulted in several intolerable situations, such as forcing unwanted children onto the streets for survival, and making the streets a safer place to be than their homes where their own parents can no longer protect them. The dream of a better life has left entire families without husbands and older children to provide the bare essentials. The hope for a better future has promoted an exodus of people willing to sacrifice it all to begin the journey to North America and the "American Dream," though they are ignorant of the perils and organized forces that are waiting to begin their recruitment based on lies. Reaching the destination has very high costs.

The demand for cheap manual labor, the need for people to work the land and in the sex industry, a trafficker's unquenchable thirst for children and women to fulfill the needs of perverts, irresponsible facilitators of adoptions, organ trafficking, servitude, and pornography are factors that make Latin American countries one of the most fertile recruiting grounds for all forms of trafficking.

I. **Causes that affect the demand of Sex Trafficking and Exploitation in Latin America**

    a. Community tolerance of prostitution based on concepts of virginity and religion [we must create an alternative way of teaching men about sex, apart from the traditional view that girls in Latin America are supposed to be kept virgins.]

    b. Survival sex for countless homeless children make easy access for recruitment

    c. Unwanted births and economic factors [trigger false adoptions]

    d. Poverty and low wages [cause migrant girls to be exploited and provided to migrant workers for sex. Children are sold even before they reach their place of destination. The U.S. exacerbates this exploitation as its (farming) industries create demand for cheap labor.]

    e. Governmental instability that leads to corruption and ignorance regarding the severity of the problem [resulting in the lack of a protective judicial system and homogenous strategies among governments.]

    f. Lack of a protective judicial system to prevent trafficking and exploitation

II. **Causes that promote demand through U.S. exploitation of trafficking services**

    a. Lack of U.S. agricultural and manual laborers

    b. Lower wages to immigrants

    c. Growing sex industry [for example, girls and boys are used for snuff films, in which the child is ultimately killed and what is left of the body parts are then sold] and other forms of organized crime [such as drug trafficking, in which drugs are put in the mouths of children and prostitutes when they are forced to cross borders.] There is corruption on both sides of the border.

    d. Restrictions on North American adoptions

    e. The acceptance of Macho behavior and irresponsibility of men's behavior [many cultures teach that the men have the right to have sex with women, and this concept of machismo is mirrored in the United States and fuels the perversion of getting "more kicks" through sex.]

    f. Sex tourism

    g. [Easy access through borders

        i. People do not know about trafficking laws. Border guards easily confuse trafficking and smuggling laws.

        ii. The military go to the other side of the border because of the variety of women, but mainly because the laws tolerate access to sexual services from women and children.]

III. **Action to minimize the demand factor**

    a. Homogenized actions targeting demand (for example, campaigns and pamphlets)

    b. Stiff penalties for pimps and pedophiles, organized crime, corruption, and strong extradition laws for those who break the laws

    c. Government treaties between Latin American countries and the U.S. on specific areas of demand

    d. Target organized crime through a network of intelligence factors

    e. A system that punishes the perpetrator and decriminalizes the victim.

It is important for each Latin American country to recognize the factors promoting the demand for trafficking and to work to eliminate them, as well as the need to create measures that will protect those who cannot protect themselves and that target organized crime in its endeavor to harm women and children.

Panel 2: Questions and Answers

[**Question: (Norma Hotaling)** It is difficult to change language and the focus of speech in communities. Prostitution brings neighbors together. They meet to discuss how to get rid of the prostitutes dirtying their neighborhood. In order to change language, people must also talk about who else is there—the men. There is no language for the men in these neighborhoods. Power and secrecy keeps attention on the women. How can we get people to change their language and understand that men are there?

Answer: (Jackson Katz) This dilemma is a concrete example of why it is important to alter our speech so that men are made visible. There is a language for men if we shift the subject from victim to the perpetrator. Instead of asking how many teenage girls get pregnant each year, ask how many young men impregnate teenage girls each year. Instead of asking how many women are raped each day, ask how many men rape women each day? Instead of asking how many prostitutes there are in the city, ask how many men patronize the services of prostitutes in the city.

Answer: (Marisa Ugarte) Community health providers are undergoing training that gives them the tools and confidence to talk about male responsibility. The focus on the awful acts that men commit against women and children bring the camaraderie of men into a negative light. For example, the military's act against pedophiles establishes that having sexual relations with a child is unacceptable, intolerable, and punishable behavior.

Answer: (Derek Ellerman) We must ask how we can change ourselves. People can be open-minded—men included. The framework of trafficking can help us think about where attention should focus, and who should be held responsible. There is more sympathy for foreign victims. People can somehow feel that a seven year old born in the land of freedom has the right to choose to enter prostitution or not. As members of the anti-trafficking committee, we must continue to foster dialogue around the issue of demand in order to perpetuate an understanding of and resistance to both domestic and international trafficking.

Answer: (Laura Lederer) Our laws are structured to protect the victim. We need to make use of this victim-centered approach within and across borders.

Comment: (Vidya Samarasinghe) We cannot completely dismiss the passive voice. The primacy in terms of supply is important because we must focus on the women and children in order to prioritize our efforts to help them. We must not only look at how demand is symbolized and nurtured (for example, by the Internet), but also about what demand actually is. There are poor men and women that go into prostitution. In general, men have disposable income and women do not. This disposable income enables men to buy the sexual services of other women, men, and children. To deconstruct demand, we must understand where the demand originates.

Response: (Marisa Ugarte) Archetypes in culture represent how behaviors change or stay constant. The medieval belief that men could claim the right to rape a woman has continued to establish a patriarchal society.

Question: (Susan Breault) When we look at the male population, we overlook teen and college-age boys, who use street services and see prostitution as a rite of passage. We need to reach these boys at the junior high level to change their attitudes and educate them about who the victim is. If school-aged boys are given the facts and taught to be held accountable for the treatment of girls and women, they will listen.

Answer: (Jackson Katz) There are tensions within the politics of these issues. In reality, proposals to bring this kind of education into schools are met with strong conservative resistance. Even anti-rape education has had a hard time getting into school because of the reluctance to discuss sex. If we cannot discuss rape, how can we even begin to talk about prostitution? Also, the triumph of market values results in our commodifying every human need, including sex. There is opposition to discussion of prostitution in schools by those who allow the market value of sex to transcend the humanistic value of human worth. Many conservatives, for example, morally oppose a behavior (prostitution), but they champion the market values that in a sense sustain it.

Answer: (Laura Lederer) We need to call attention to rape, prostitution, and trafficking through the framework of the intrinsic worth of a woman and child and human dignity. Conservatives would be more willing to become our allies.

Comment: (Steven Wagner) As a social conservative, I would not permit someone to come into my son's school to talk against rape. I would let you come into my son's school to talk about how objectification of women diminishes men's masculinity.

Response: (Jackson Katz) There is no difference between these two topics. Rape prevention, in part, is about how certain patriarchal constructions of masculinity lead to rape and how traditional concepts of "manhood" keep a lot of men silent.

Question: (Karin Brandenburg) Has the volume of demand over the last 25 years increased? In other words, are foreign victims replacing national victims, or is the number of domestic victims remaining stable while foreign victims are increased in order to respond to (or even create) an increase in demand?

Answer: (Derek Ellerman) In some sectors, domestic networks are being replaced. For example, Korean networks have replaced many open brothels that were run by Italian-American networks. Generally, however, increased demand is forcing supply networks into areas that were previously untouched. The Internet is one explanation for the increase in demand in certain sectors.

Comment: (Melissa Farley) It is important to have men speak about their experiences with friends in order to cut into the silence and complicity that surrounds violence against women. Organizing a speak-out would create a safe setting for men to share what they know and feel about prostitution. We can learn so much about men and what they go through by talking to them about their experiences. It is imperative to understand that silence is backed by a threat of violence. The experience of a friend demonstrates that many men fear physical repercussions if they stand against their peers. The friend attended a bachelor party in which the men hired a prostitute. He did not feel comfortable with their treatment of the woman. He, therefore, quietly attempted to leave the party. The act of leaving made him fear that he would be beaten. Men's silence is founded upon a realistic fear that speaking out would jeopardize their safety.

Response: (Jackson Katz) We must create a big tent for men working to end men's violence against women.

Question: (Sandra Hunnicutt) It is very effective to name those that have not been named through our use of the active voices. Can the U.S. government implement the active voice into its language?

Answer: (Laura Lederer) Yes, the language can be implemented; we are at a crossroads in the formation of U.S. policy. There is a critical mass of people forming a broad-based coalition, and it is up to us, as part of this coalition, to tell the State Department what we want. The State Department relies on expertise to determine policy. We must send letters demanding that the link between prostitution and trafficking be addressed and the active voice be adopted. There will be money for research so that intervention programs can be designed and implemented.

Question: (Ruth Pojman) Demand can be artificially created. Demand is shoved in our faces in hotels and through pop-up internet advertisements. There is no innate demand for laptop dancing. Influences, such as peer pressure, foster the idea that demand can be excused by our natural propensity for sex. Is there really an innate demand for sex?

Answer: (Derek Ellerman) All of these influences stimulate demand. For example, internet pornography get men addicted for free, they become hooked, and they go to other sources to satisfy their cravings. Pornography sites and dealers have expanded the sex industry by ensnaring more buyers.

Answer: (Laura Lederer) Demand can be artificially created.

Question: (Kaethe Morris Hoffer) Do newspapers ever get asked if they are aware that they are advertising for the sex industry?

Answer: (Derek Ellerman) The newspapers have been confronted and have met with law enforcement. They argue that if they forbid the advertisements, they would be accused of discriminating against a specific community, such as the Koreans.

Question: (Kristin Houser) The newspapers know that they are advertising where a person can go to serially rape a woman or a child. Has anyone ever charged these publishers with aiding and abetting?

Answer: (Derek Ellerman) It is difficult to go against powerhouses such as the *Washington Post*. It is important to convince prosecutors and rally against politicians supporting the newspapers.

Question: (Kaethe Morris Hoffer) Research conducted in 2002 found that there are 16,000 prostitutes in Chicago. If there are this many women, how many men have consumed their services? Is there a ratio that would be a useful multiplier of prostitutes to johns?

Answer: (Marisa Ugarte) A prostitute in San Diego can service twenty to thirty men in ten hours.

Comment: (Donna Hughes) The term "gendered violence" covers up the reality of violence against women because there is no distinction between the victim and the perpetrator. Men's violence against women is most definitive.

Response: (Jackson Katz) I agree, but the term is sometimes a little too clunky. Also, the term "gender violence" is a more inclusive term than "men's violence against women," which, incidentally, I use most of the time. There is a growing momentum among men to do this work. More men are doing this work today than ten to twenty years ago. We know that women are the leaders of this work, but men want to build off this and work collaboratively with women.

Comment: (Twiss Butler) Some men are resistant to taking a stance against prostitution because they themselves do not go to a prostitute or look at pornography on the Internet. We need to meet this resistance with dialogue that explains that there is a payoff off for all men when women are subjugated and male domination is maintained. For example, we acknowledge that even when an individual person is not racist, he or she receives a payoff from those that are racist because his or her race becomes privileged.

Comment: (Mary Anne Layden) Rip out the pages of the phonebooks in hotel rooms that advertise escort services as a small protest against the sex industry. The Omni Hotels have removed the pornography channels in all rooms across the country. They are losing millions of dollars; we must express our gratitude and appreciation.

Question: (Unidentified speaker) Besides encouraging men to take a stand against pornography, prostitution, and trafficking, we need to pressure the police and the criminal justice system that protects the consumers. Many law enforcers say that they are not going to waste their resources on men because men are the real victims and the pimps are the true abusers. If police actually choose to prosecute someone other than the prostitute, they will go after the black man on the street because they mistakenly see the pimp as the only dangerous factor in her life. They do not apply the law that exists on the book that could be used to protect women and children. For example, police could charge a john with statutory rape if he has sex with a minor. The criminal justice system is condoning the rape of young girls and thus creates demand.

Answer: (Derek Ellerman) Male peer culture is pervasive. There is tremendous pressure in the police department to look the other way and not treat the women as victims. Male peer culture tells them to see prostitutes as the ones soliciting sex from men and to view prostitution as a way of life of that women choose. Police departments are responsive to community action. It is possible, therefore, to protect the true victims.]

Panel 3:
What Governmental Policies or Practices Enable the Actions of Those Who Create Demand?[1]

Moderator: Vidyamali Samarasinghe

Anti-trafficking strategies, especially in the case of female sex trafficking, normally focus more on supply for a number of very good reasons, chief among which is the recognition of the traumatic experiences of a vulnerable group of people, namely girls and women. However, the problem of female sex trafficking could never be solved unless and until we focus our attention on the demand sector. Without demand, tackling prostitution and trafficking is "like trying to trap a fly with one hand." It seems to me that for the most part people have been intimidated away from discussing demand and strategizing to combat demand. The first question to ask is: who consumes prostitution? What does demand look like? What are the agencies and institutions that help to encourage the demand for prostitution?

Governments play a critical role in focusing on demand. There are three "P's" that are essential to fighting trafficking: prevention, protection of victims, and prosecution of traffickers. Governments take on the responsibility, in most instances, for the protection of trafficking victims. They have the sole responsibility for the prosecution of traffickers. Towards this end, governments pass legislation, enforce laws, and are expected to ensure that the law enforcement and the judiciary are made aware of the problems and remedies of trafficking. However,

---

[1] Bracketed comments are summaries provided by Sara Dubin, Sarah James, Pavana Bhat, and Heena Musabji.

it is important to note that government efforts to protect victims and prosecute perpetrators of trafficking by themselves would be insufficient to "prevent" female sex trafficking.

A majority of the females who are victims of trafficking end up as prostitutes. As the demand for prostitutes increase, there will be an increase in the incidence of females trafficked to supply this highly profitable economic activity. It is well known that in some developing countries governments actually play a role that triggers prostitution. They encourage organizations that enable prostitution, such as tourism and entertainment. These are industries that create large revenues. Prostitution is the most profitable tourist attraction in Thailand and the Philippines. Hence, governments often encourage female sex trafficking by turning a blind eye to the "use" of women and girls for the purpose of entertainment for tourists who bring in foreign currency revenue to the countries. In many countries, prostitution is illegal. However, these illegal activities are often overlooked. Hence, it is important that we identify government practices and policies that encourage organizations and institutions to traffic women and girls into prostitution.

There are various government approaches around the world that encourage and tolerate prostitution. Scotland has adopted "tolerance zones," where prostitution is "tolerated." Accordingly, reports indicate that in Edinburgh prostitution is prevalent and foreign women are often trafficked to feed the industry. However, in Glasgow feminist groups are challenging the establishment of tolerance zones. In Australia, before prostitution was legalized, there were sixty to seventy brothels in Victoria, but after legalization, there were over 100. Street prostitution also doubled. This is yet another strategy by which the government protects the profitable sex trade and denies that there are any trafficking problems, *i.e.,* it says it has an illegal immigrant problem, not a trafficking problem. However, since the death of a woman in detention who was trafficked, Australian government is paying some attention to the issue of trafficking for prostitution. In Europe, the EU has recognized prostitution as a job requiring a work permit. Legalized prostitution in the Netherlands makes up five percent of the economy.

Some governments claim that since it cannot stop demand, they might as well regulate prostitution by requiring brothel keepers to comply with health and safety regulations. When inspectors arrive, the trafficked women disappear to escort services or onto the streets. Many women do not want to register as prostitutes because they believe they will only be doing it for a short while.

Legalization is being discussed in the Czech Republic, Thailand, and Taiwan. Legalizing prostitution does not seem to stop trafficking. Furthermore, governments should play a proactive role in preempting the incidence of trafficking by going beyond prosecutions to combat trafficking.

Panelist: Kenneth Franzblau

Equality Now

I believe that the demand for trafficked persons is enabled by policies of inaction and the lack of procedures that recognize the relationship between activities such as prostitution, sex tourism, pornography and trafficking. The relationship between these demand activities and trafficking has already been recognized in the Trafficking Victims Protection Act of 2000; by the Trafficking in Persons National Security Directive of February, 2003; by John Miller, Director of the Office to Monitor and Combat Trafficking in Persons; and the proposed Trafficking Victims Protection Reauthorization Act of 2003. We now need to convert that recognition into policies and practices to be implemented by all levels of government. These policies should provide for stricter law enforcement and have a strong educational component about trafficking, prostitution -related activities, and their effects on victims.

The failure to address the solicitation and patronizing of adult women in prostitution in foreign countries by U.S. residents is a serious policy failing. The Department of Defense should adopt and strictly enforce a worldwide zero-tolerance policy on the solicitation of prostitution by U.S. military personnel. National Security Presidential Directive twenty-two states that "the United States Government opposes prostitution and any related activities." Our commitment to this policy will be questioned, however, if brothels using trafficked women continue to be created immediately next to U.S. military bases. Ultimately, if U.S. military personnel increase the demand for trafficked women, our assessments of other countries' efforts to combat trafficking will become subject to the same criticism as our drug certification process did in the 1990s.

The brothels and bars that open in response to the demand created by U.S. military personnel, and the experiences of U.S. military personnel in those establishments, also serve as the foundation of the sex tourism industry. History shows that sex tourism follows the flag. Popular sex tour destinations, such as Angeles City and Olongapo in the Philippines, were once the sites of large U.S. military installations. And, U.S.-based sex tour operators, in their advertising, frequently mention their sexual exploits in the service.

Given the U.S. government's recognition of the relationship between sex tourism, prostitution, and trafficking, the Department of Justice should consider Mann Act prosecutions of sex tour operators. The plain language of the Mann Act makes it a crime to transport a person in foreign or interstate commerce intending for them to "engage in prostitution or in any sexual activity for which any person can be charged with a criminal offense." Since patronizing and prostitution is illegal in most sex tour destinations, sex tourists and the women they get sex from could be charged with criminal offenses. A Mann Act violation by sex tour operators, therefore, exists.

Recent Trafficking Victims Protection Act (Protect Act) amendments create additional opportunities to prosecute sex tour operators and sex tourists. It is no longer necessary for prosecutors to prove that foreign travel was undertaken with the intent to have sex with a minor. Proof of the commission of such an act is sufficient in and of itself. When G & F Tours turns its customers loose on the bargirls of Bangkok or Angeles City, they will inevitably have sex with a minor unless you believe that none of these girls are under eighteen. To quote Norman Barabash, the ugly operator of Big Apple Oriental Tours, about the age of the women his customers patronize, "we really don't know. Short of giving them lie-detector tests, who can tell?" I would submit that the situational child abuser that the Protect Act makes subject to prosecution is likely to be found on a sex tour.

I think we also need a statutory amendment that would make it illegal to travel in foreign commerce and engage in any commercial sex act. What credible political, moral, or public policy argument exists in favor of U.S. residents being able to travel to other countries and purchase sex? At a time when our government is expending substantial resources to improve the image of the U.S., we should not be undermining those efforts by permitting stereotypical "Ugly Americans" to take advantage of the poverty and oppression of others.

It would also be a good practice to consider a country's effort toward criminalizing and enforcing its laws on soliciting, patronizing, and pimping when assessing their efforts to combat trafficking as provided by the Trafficking Victims Protection Act of 2000. The ability to do so should already exist pursuant to that section of the statute that permits the Secretary of State to consider other information relating to trafficking that he deems appropriate when making those assessments. Having repeatedly acknowledged the demand for trafficked women created by prostitution and sex tourism, I do not believe we can ignore them when assessing a country's anti-trafficking efforts.

It should also be the policy of the United States to aggressively promote the equality of women in its dealings with countries deficient in this area. I do not believe that a country that denies women their basic human rights will act to suppress the demand for trafficked women. For example, the State Department's 2002 Country Report on Human Rights Practices for Saudi Arabia sets forth a laundry list of violations of women's rights that goes on for almost two full pages. These include lack of political and social rights, prohibitions against driving, restrictions on using public facilities, and the inability to travel abroad without the approval of their husband. I do not find it surprising then that the State Department's 2003 Trafficking in Persons Report finds that Saudi Arabia is a destination country for trafficking victims.

Nor do we do a much better job of addressing the promotion, solicitation, and patronizing of prostitution here. At the local level, the policies and practices that enable the demand for trafficked women are enabled by incorrect assumptions: (1) the acceptance that prostitution is the world's oldest or second oldest profession; it's not a profession at all; (2) the belief that prostitution is a victimless crime; and (3) the idea that prostitution can be addressed as a zoning or public nuisance situation.

Attitudes such as these, which in my experience are fairly wide spread, result in police departments making prostitution offenses a low-priority concern, misdirect the focus that does exist towards arresting the woman and not those that patronize or pimp them, and creates a professional cycle of neglect so that new officers do not receive training in prostitution-related crimes and that efforts in those areas are not seen as an asset in career advancement.

If the professional interest of law enforcement towards prostitution stops with the arrest of prostituted women, they will not learn about the demand for trafficked women created by those who patronize prostitutes. And it is my belief that at the level of municipal police work there is a dangerous lack of knowledge about trafficking, the abuse suffered by trafficking victims, and how prostitution in its myriad forms (brothels, strip clubs and massage parlors) fuel the demand for trafficked women.

Last week, I had a conversation with a lieutenant in a suburban New York Police Department. It is a small department but with adequate resources and proximity to New York City. I asked him what he knew about the Trafficking Victims Protection Act. "Nothing" he said. I asked what he knew about the trafficking of persons for commercial sex or forced labor. He said, "What I see on TV." I asked if his department had received any information on trafficking of persons. He checked their bulletins and advisories and told me they had not.

I suppose you could write this off by saying, "Well, what's the big deal. What are the chances of someone being trafficked to suburban New York." But I think we need to treat this as important because we know that trafficking victims do not wind up only in large cities. We also know that trafficking, by its very definition, means that its victims will be moved through suburban and rural areas. And as Derek [Ellerman] informed us yesterday, if there are not going to be pro-active federal investigations into trafficking, then cases will have to be created at the point of first contact, local police. And if police do not know what they are looking for or cannot recognize a trafficking situation when it presents itself, then we are in deep trouble indeed.

At a minimum, local law enforcement and government agencies with the power to act against demand-related activities should not facilitate the process. For instance, the State of Hawaii has granted a travel agent's license to a gentleman named Melvin Hamaguchi, who runs the "Ultimate Asian Sex Tour" to Thailand. This is the name of his company that appears on his website. In August 2002, Equality Now filed a complaint with Hawaii's Regulated Industries Complaint Office seeking to have his license revoked. Our complaint included emails from Hamaguchi making it clear that he was promoting prostitution in violation of Hawaii's penal code. Our complaint was closed by the state agency because it claimed the agency could only revoke a travel agent's license in cases of fraud or deception. So, if I went on an Ultimate Asian Sex Tour and didn't have a threesome or didn't get sex with a different woman every day as promised by Mr. Hamaghuchi, then there would be grounds to have his license revoked. But if he merely promotes prostitution in violation of Hawaii's and Thailand's laws or even if he facilitated sex with a minor, the State of Hawaii would not move against his license. Although the complaint was re-opened, Mr. Hamaguchi will be leading another sex tour to Thailand in three weeks' time.

I believe that there are polices and practices that can be implemented at the local level, some with federal assistance, to educate police about the relationship between the demand for prostituted women and trafficking. While this is to some extent my personal wish list, for the most part these policies require will and not a great expenditure of funds. These policies and practices include:

1. All courses for basic police certification, supervisory certification, and police department accreditation should include training about the abuses of women in prostitution; the necessity of investigation and arresting johns and pimps; how the activities of these two groups contribute to the demand for trafficked women; and how to identify trafficking situations.

2. Federal assistance to local law enforcement agencies should be conditioned upon the recipient putting in place zero-tolerance policies for pimping and patronizing and requiring notification to relevant federal agencies and social service providers where trafficking is suspected.

3. The FBI National Academy, in its program for local police personnel, should include training in trafficking and the Trafficking Victims Protection Act, as well as the relationship between patronizing, pimping, and the demand for trafficked women.

4. Every police officer in America should be provided with copies of the pamphlets, "Trafficking in Persons Guide for Non-Governmental Organizations" and "Information for Victims of Trafficking in Persons and Forced Labor" through their employers Even such basic information would be a quantum leap over what is now being received at the local level.

5. The Federal Government should attempt to provide experienced anti-trafficking personnel for training local law enforcement agencies.

6. Private law enforcement training organizations should be encouraged to provide training on trafficking and demand-related activities. Of 106 courses listed on the "policetraining.net" schedule between October 13 and 31, 2003, none dealt with trafficking and only two seemed likely to have any relevance to crimes such as patronizing or pimping.
7. States should adopt anti-trafficking legislation.
8. States should amend their statutes to provide for asset seizure and forfeiture in patronizing and pimping cases with seized assets divided equally between the state, the seizing agency, and rehabilitation programs for women seeking to leave prostitution.
9. There should be increased provision of and funding for "John Schools" for first-time patronizers of women in prostitution.

Even in countries where women enjoy statutory equality, we often see cultural and social practices that objectify women and make the pursuit of prostitution, pornography, and sex tourism acceptable. The multi-billion dollar pornography industry in the U.S. broadcasts directly into our homes, is available at virtually every stationery store and newsstand, and is unavoidable on the Internet. Business meetings are held in strip clubs without objection. The "mainstream media" bombards us with uncountable close-ups of the female anatomy in music videos, moronic prime time programming, like the Man Show, and the frat-boy literary content of Maxim. If the number of killings children see on television desensitizes them to violence, how can the way women are portrayed result in their being seen as anything other than objects of sexual gratification by young boys and male adolescents?

Perhaps it is time to figure out how to take the lessons taught at SAGE's John School and convert them into curriculum for middle school and high school health classes. I fear that if we do not educate boys about the violence of prostitution and pornography and how women are trafficked to satisfy the demand they create, we will never defeat the form of slavery that is human trafficking.

Panelist: Donna M. Hughes

Governmental Approaches to the Demand for Prostitution: The Emergence of the New Abolitionist Movement

Introduction

Trafficking for prostitution is a global problem that occurs in every region of the world, with women and children being trafficked to, from, or through every country of the world.[2] The flow of women and children from sending to receiving countries is characterized as a balance between supply and demand.[3] Factors influencing the supply of women from sending countries include poverty, unemployment, and lack of a promising future. Criminals, organized crime networks, and corrupt officials in the sending countries and receiving countries prey upon this pool of women looking for work and opportunities abroad.[4] The supply side of trafficking has received most of the attention of researchers, NGOs, and policy makers. Until recently, less attention was paid to the demand side of trafficking.

Now, there is a global debate on "the demand." Does an increase in the number of women and children in prostitution in destination countries cause an increase in the demand for trafficked women and children from sending countries? Over the past decade, a number of governments and organizations have questioned whether trafficking and prostitution are linked. There is general acceptance that trafficking is harmful and should be criminalized, but there is a debate about prostitution between those who want to regulate it and those who want to abolish it. As sex industries and the trafficking of women and children increase in destination countries, there is increasing debate on how governments should respond.

---

[2] Donna M. Hughes, "The 'Natasha' Trade: The Transnational Shadow Market of Trafficking in Women," *Journal of International Affairs*, Spring 2000, Vol. 53, No.2, pp. 625-651.

[3] Donna M. Hughes, "Men Create the Demand, Women Are the Supply," Lecture on Sexual Exploitation, *World Forum on Violence Against Women*, Queen Sofia Center, Valencia, Spain, 26 November 2000.

[4] Donna M. Hughes and Tatyana A. Denisova, "The Transnational Political Criminal Nexus of Trafficking of Women in Ukraine," *Trends in Organized Crime*, Vol. 6, No. 3-4: Spr.-Sum. 2001.

In destination countries, the legal status of types of sexual exploitation, such as prostitution, pornography, and stripping, varies from being legal to partially legal to illegal, depending on the destination country. The size of the legal or illegal operations determines the number of women and children that are needed to maintain their operations. States have set different philosophical and policy approaches towards prostitution. Currently, there are three general approaches to prostitution: tolerance, regulation, and abolition.

Tolerance Approaches

In the tolerance approach, states tolerate prostitution and do not attempt to regulate or prohibit it in an effective way. Tolerance is created in three ways: 1) there are no laws concerning prostitution; 2) the laws are weak, ineffective, and therefore seldom used; or 3) there is no enforcement of existing laws. The best examples of tolerant or unregulated environment are in the countries of the former Soviet Union. Before the collapse of the Soviet Union, there was little prostitution and the closed borders prevented transnational trafficking. Within ten years following the opening up of the borders, hundreds of thousands of women and children had been trafficked out of the countries of the former Soviet Union for prostitution all over the world. Western Europe and East Asia, particularly Japan and Korea, were popular destinations. Although less well known, women and children are trafficked into Russian cities, such as Moscow and St. Petersburg. Today, there are an estimated 100,000 women in prostitution in Moscow, 80 percent of them from the former Soviet republics or rural areas of Russia.

Russia has a tolerant or unregulated approach to prostitution and trafficking. There is no law against the trafficking of women and children. Laws against pimping and procuring are weak and ineffective. Prostitution is an administrative offense.[5] The proliferation of prostitution and trafficking in Russia is an example of what happens in a tolerant or unregulated environment in which traffickers and pimps are undeterred from recruiting women and children and selling them abroad or in metropolitan areas.

In other parts of the world, local municipalities have adopted a tolerance approach by setting aside certain sections of cities to be "tol-

---

[5] The Russian Federation is likely to pass an anti-trafficking law and amend the criminal code to make pimping and procuring felonies before the end of 2003.

erance zones," in which prostitution will be allowed. Amsterdam in the Netherlands and Edinburgh in Scotland have street areas dedicated to allowing prostitution.[6] The "tolerance zone" approach is being debated in many cities on several continents.

Regulation Approaches

When prostitution and trafficking proliferate and are judged to be "out of control," especially street prostitution that offends the public, legalization or regulation of prostitution is often suggested as a solution. Those who promote legalization claim it will "clean up" the business, and get the women off the street and out of sight of the public.

That has not proven to be the case in Australia, which has legalized prostitution in select states, such as Victoria. According to researchers in Australia, before legalization there were between 60 and 70 illegal massage parlors in Victoria. Now, there are 100 legal brothels and an estimated 400 illegal ones. And the street prostitution problem has doubled: one area has gone from having 150 women on the street to 350.[7]

Legalized prostitution has also enabled the creation of large brothels. The Daily Planet in Melbourne was an illegal brothel for 13 years before the state of Victoria legalized prostitution in 1984. It is the first brothel to trade on the stock market. It takes 150 women to keep the Daily Planet operating to serve the 900 men who visit each week. The proprietor of The Daily Planet in Australia is planning on building franchises in 15 other countries, including the U.S., where he is planning a sexual theme park near Las Vegas.[8]

Legalized prostitution in Australia has led the government to protect its now taxpaying, profitable sex industry. Although there are thousands of foreign women in the brothels of Australia, most of them from Asian countries such as Thailand and the Philippines, the gov-

---

[6] "On the streets of Edinburgh, a benign view of prostitution," *The Guardian*, December 30, 2003; Lara Macmillan, "Is Edinburgh becoming the sex capital?" *Edinburgh Evening News*, 10 June 2002; Mijntje Klipp, "Pick-up zone must close once every while," *Het Parool* , August 17, 2002; Bas Kromhout, "Tippelzone* comes apart at the seams," *Street News the Hague*, September 2002.

[7] Lorna Martin, "Is this the future of sex?" *The Herald* (UK), 7 May 2003.

[8] Id.

71

ernment of Australia has steadfastly denied that it has a trafficking problem. Australia only acknowledges having an illegal immigrant problem. The violence and coercion are ignored.

The Netherlands took the regulation approach to the demand. The Dutch believed that it is not possible to decrease the demand, so the best approach is to regulate it; prostitution and brothels were legalized in 2000. As the Netherlands moved towards legalization, it became increasingly tolerant of prostitution and the sex industry grew. In the last decade, it has increased 25 percent.[9] The Dutch government has also received a judgment from the European Court recognizing prostitution as an economic activity, thus enabling women from outside the European Union to obtain work permits to be "sex workers" in the Dutch sex industry. The sex industry is now a $1 billion business. Research before legalization found that 80 percent of the women in brothels in the Netherlands were trafficked[10] from over 32 different countries.[11]

Since legalization, brothel keepers have had to comply with health and safety requirements, and the women and brothel keepers have to pay taxes. When inspectors started coming to the brothels, all the foreign trafficked women disappeared. This has led to vacancies in the brothels that the owners have had difficulty filling because local women do not want or have to do this "work."[12] Although illegal foreign women are now rarely found in registered brothels, they are still being used in prostitution in the Netherlands. The traffickers and pimps moved out of the legal brothels and opened escort services using cell phones from apartments or moved women to the street in places called

---

[9] Suzanne Daley, "New rights for Dutch prostitutes, but no gain," *New York Times*, 12 Aug 2001.

[10] Budapest Group, "The relationship between organized crime and trafficking in aliens," Austria: International Centre for Migration Policy Development, June 1999.

[11] International Organization for Migration, "Trafficking and Prostitution: The Growing Exploitation of Migrant Women from Central and Eastern Europe," May 1995.

[12] "Sex vacancy," *De Volkskrant*, 13 April 2002, p. 24.

tippelzones.[13] The trafficked women, mostly from Eastern Europe and Western Africa, are still controlled by pimps and traffickers.[14]

There is evidence from countries that have legalized prostitution that legalization leads to growth and expansion of the sex industry–with the accompanying demand for more women. Where do the women come from? Do more local women sign up? No; in every case, more women are trafficked from Asia, Eastern Europe, or Africa to meet the demand. There is no indication that regulation approaches have decreased trafficking.

Strict regulation of prostitution is unpopular with the pimps because there are too many regulations and they have to pay taxes. They prefer an open, unregulated and tolerant environment.[15] Also, women in prostitution do not like the regulated approach because they have to register, thereby creating an official record that they were prostitutes.

Among advocates of so-called "sex worker rights" there is a movement away from supporting legalization to supporting decriminalization, meaning remove all criminal penalties from prostitution, procuring, pimping, and brothel keeping, but impose few regulations. New Zealand has just adopted this approach. New Zealand has decriminalized prostitution at the national level and left regulation of prostitution and brothels up to local authorities.

Abolitionist Approaches

There are two approaches to eradicating prostitution: prohibition and abolition. In the U.S., with the exception of a few counties in Nevada, we have a prohibition approach at the local level, meaning that all activities related to prostitution are criminalized: soliciting, procuring, pimping, and brothel keeping. There is no differentiation between victims and perpetrators. There is little support for the prohibitionist approach today.

---

[13] Anja Sligter, "Open air brothel," *De Volkskrant*, July 24, 2002; "Tippelzone comes apart at the seams," Street news the Hague, *Bas Kromhout*, September 2002.

[14] "More trafficking in women since lifting of brothel ban," *Reformatisch Dagblad*, 22 August 2002.

[15] "Brothel keeper prefers to remain illegal," *De volkskrant*, 20 June 2002.

Two countries have adopted an abolitionist approach and are leading what can be called a new abolitionist movement: Sweden and the U.S. at the federal level. The U.S. and Sweden have conceptualized the problem of trafficking and prostitution in slightly different ways, but the impact of their approaches is similar.

In Sweden, beginning in 1999, the purchasing of sexual services became a crime. The law was passed as part of a new violence against women act that broadened the activities that qualified as criminal acts of violence. With this new approach, "prostitution is considered to be one of the most serious expressions of the oppression of and discrimination against women." The focus of the law is on "the demand" or the behavior of the "purchasers," not the women.[16] According to the Deputy Prime Minister of Sweden, Margareta Winberg, "the international prostitution debate has tended, for very good reasons, to focus on the women, who, for one reason or another have been drawn into prostitution. Today, however, we can see where the true problem lies – it lies with the buyers, the customers, the men."[17]

As a result of the new law in Sweden, open prostitution in the streets has been significantly reduced. The law has had a disruptive effect on men seeking to buy sexual services, reducing that activity by almost 80 percent. Foreign women, who are likely to be victims of trafficking, have disappeared from the streets.[18] Prostitution still exists; the pimps have moved to more clandestine venues, such as apartments and escort services. Sweden is also using its foreign aid to promote this abolitionist approach in other countries, particularly in the Nordic Baltic region.

As I said earlier, the U.S., with the exception of several counties in Nevada, has a prohibitionist approach to prostitution. These are state and local laws, not federal laws. There is no federal law on prostitution. There is a federal law called the Mann Act, passed in 1911, that criminalizes the interstate transportation of persons for purpose of pros-

---

[16] Karin Grundberg, "Sweden's prostitutes ply their trade on the Internet, *Agence France Presse* , Jan 13, 2003.

[17] Margareta Winberg, Deputy Prime Minister of Sweden, Keynote speech; "Pathbreaking Strategies in the Global Fight Against Sex Trafficking," 24 February 2003, Hyatt Regency Hotel, Washington D.C., USA.

[18] Ingmarie Froman, "Sweden's fight against trafficking in women," Swedish Institute, 14 May 2003.

titution. It criminalizes the internal trafficking of persons. That law is still used today. In fact, in almost every state and locality, the U.S. has good laws that criminalize the demand and organization of prostitution. These activities include recruiting, pimping, running a brothel, and transporting victims for the purpose of prostitution. If they enforced these laws more vigorously, local authorities could have an impact on curbing the demand for prostitution and the accompanying trafficking of women and children.

There have been efforts to address specifically the demand in the U.S. Some municipalities have added extra penalties for men who solicit women for prostitution by confiscating their cars, printing their names in newspapers, and placing their names and photos on websites. One successful effort to combat the demand in the U.S. is the First Offender Program, commonly known as the John's School, run by SAGE in San Francisco. This program specifically provides men who have been arrested with education about the harm and health risks of prostitution.

In the U.S., at the federal level, the approach to prostitution is moving towards an abolitionist position. In 2000, the U.S. Congress passed the Trafficking Victims Protection Act (TVPA) 2000, which takes aim at the traffickers of foreign nationals and provides relief and services to victims of trafficking. The TVPA, which is abolitionist in its approach, was opposed by the Clinton administration, which was pushing for a regulationist approach. Earlier this year, the U.S. issued the first opinion on the link between prostitution and trafficking. President George W. Bush issued a National Security Presidential Directive that links prostitution to trafficking: "Prostitution and related activities, which are inherently harmful and dehumanizing, contribute to the phenomenon of trafficking in persons..."[19] This policy statement is important because it relinks trafficking and prostitution and states that prostitution is harmful. This policy goes against the regulationist approach that delinks prostitution and trafficking and accepts that prostitution can be a form of work that can be regulated.

Congress and a number of federal agencies have followed President Bush's direction in setting new policies that oppose trafficking and the regulation of prostitution. In March 2003, the U.S. Agency for International Development (USAID) released a policy on funding. It states "Organizations advocating prostitution as an employment

---

[19] Trafficking in Persons National Security Presidential Directive, 25 February 2003.

choice or which advocate or support the legalization of prostitution are not appropriate partners for USAID anti-trafficking grants or contracts."

The U.S. Department of State adopted this policy perspective in October 2003:

> U.S. non-governmental organizations, and their sub-grantees, cannot use U.S. Government funds to lobby for, promote, or advocate the legalization or regulation of prostitution as a legitimate form of work. Foreign non-governmental organizations, and their sub-grantees, that receive U.S. Government funds to fight trafficking in persons cannot lobby for, promote, or advocate the legalization or regulation of prostitution as a legitimate form of work. It is the responsibility of the primary grantee to ensure these criteria are met by its sub-grantees.

Also in October, the U.S. Department of Justice released a report on trafficking of persons in the U.S. which included a similar policy statement.[20]

The U.S. Congress approved the $14 billion Global AIDS Bill (the United States Leadership Against HIV/AIDS, Tuberculosis, and Malaria Act of 2003) with the provision that all organizations that want funding from this source will have to sign statements that they oppose the legalization of prostitution:

> No funds made available to carry out this Act, or any amendment made by this Act, may be used to promote or advocate the legalization or practice of prostitution or sex trafficking.... No funds made available to carry out this Act, or any amendment made by this Act, may be used to provide assistance to any group or organization that does not have a policy explicitly opposing prostitution and sex trafficking.

These policy statements put the U.S. firmly in the abolitionist camp.

The U.S. is also moving against the sexual exploitation of women by U.S. military personnel. In May 2002, Fox News did an undercover investigation of trafficking and prostitution in South Korea.

---

[20] U.S. Department of Justice, "Assessment of U.S. Activities to Combat Trafficking in Persons," August 2003.

Fox News documented U.S. soldiers visiting establishments where there were trafficked women from Russia and the Philippines in prostitution. In the news program, military personnel who knew that the women were trafficked were interviewed.

As a result of this expose, members of Congress wrote to the Secretary of Defense demanding an investigation of trafficking of women around U.S. bases in South Korea and anywhere else U.S. military personnel are located.[21]

The Office of the Inspector General of the Department of Defense carried out an investigation of trafficking around U.S. military bases in South Korea and the Balkans. As a result, the head of U.S. forces in South Korea took the following actions: 1) 660 establishments suspected of involvement in trafficking or prostitution were declared off limits to all military personnel in Korea, 2) an education campaign to teach soldiers about trafficking and the U.S. laws against trafficking was initiated, 3) military leadership will work to improve and strengthen relations and contacts with Korean National Police to investigate prostitution and trafficking near U.S. bases, and 4) the military will improve living and recreational facilities for servicemen so they will have other recreation options.[22]

An additional report on trafficking in the Balkans and the involvement of the U.S. military in creating a demand for prostitution is underway.

President Bush has recently spoken out in ways that move the abolitionist movement forward. His speech at the United Nations on September 23, 2003, included significant remarks about the sex trade, which he called a "special evil." He was clear in his condemnation of "those who create these victims and profit from their suffering" and called for them to be severely punished. It was interesting that he used the term "sex trade" and not trafficking. Dorchen Leidholdt, in her keynote address, reminded us that when feminists first started using the term "trafficking," we meant all forms of commercial sexual exploita-

---

[21] Letter to Secretary of Defense Donald H. Rumsfeld signed by the following Members of Congress: Christopher H. Smith, Dennis Kucinich, George Voinovich, Steny Hoyer, Frank Wolf, Tom Lantos, Robert Aderholt, Joe Pitts, Melissa Hart, Mike Pence, Marcy Kaptur, Cynthia McKinney, and Diane Watson.

[22] Program Integrity Directorate, Office of Deputy Inspector General for Investigations, "Assessment of DOD Efforts to Combat Trafficking in Persons, Phase I – United States Forces Korea," August 2003.

tion, all buying, selling, and marketing of women's bodies, including using women in pornography. Since then, trafficking has acquired legal meanings, and the definition of trafficking has been considerably narrowed. So, I think it is significant that President Bush talked about the "sex trade" and not just trafficking or slavery. To me, this means he has opened up the whole issue and fight against the commercial sexual exploitation of women again. President Bush also made specific reference to "the demand": "Those who patronize this industry debase themselves and deepen the misery of others."

In the U.S., we now have good laws and policies; the next step is implementation. One of the biggest problems right now is funding; very little of U.S. government funding is going to groups that explicitly support these new abolitionist policies.

Sweden and the U.S. both have abolitionist approaches, but are coming at the problem of prostitution from different political perspectives. Sweden characterizes itself as having a feminist government, and it has conceptualized prostitution as a form of violence against women. The U.S. base of support for an abolitionist approach comes from radical feminists, conservatives, and faith-based activists. The radical feminists are in agreement with the rationale used by Sweden that prostitution is a form of violence against women, while the conservative and faith-based groups view prostitution as a violation of the dignity and well-being of women and children, the family, and society.

More sexual assault and domestic service providers are becoming involved in the anti-trafficking, anti-prostitution movement. Whether they know it or not, they understand the abolitionist approach. It is the same approach they have to sexual and domestic violence. They work from the perspective that criminal acts of violence, such as battering, rape, and incest, should be prevented, and if they are committed, the perpetrator should be appropriately punished. They do not accommodate batterers, rapists, or child molesters, or say that rape, battering, and abuse should be regulated. They say they should be abolished.

Politically, the breadth of support from such diverse camps for the abolitionist approach adds strength to the abolitionist movement—and puts pressure on the sexual liberals from the political left and the right. We need to appreciate and support the diversity of approaches and rationales for criticizing prostitution and trafficking and the harm they do. Different perspectives add richness to the analysis of why prostitution and trafficking hurt everyone they touch and why they should not be tolerated in any free, democratic society that values human rights.

A coalition of approaches to defeat the demand and provide assistance for victims gives us greater resistance against those that defend the sexual exploitation of women and children—the sexual liberals, the criminals who want to be transformed into legal businesspeople, the greedy governmental bureaucrats who are counting the tax income, and the corrupt officials. Broad based support for an abolitionist movement will enable use to engage in a more successful fight against trafficking and the sexual exploitation of women and children.

[Dr. Samarasinghe ended Panel 3 with questions to consider for discussion:

Would legalization end all efforts? What else could be done? How do you follow it up?

In a globalized world in which some third world countries are trying to legalize prostitution, what is it in the legalization process that is so wrong?

How can we make regulations stick in terms of global sex tourism? Domestic regulations are not enough; we need harmonization of legal process.

How do we build coalitions to get funding from governments (as in the example of the U.S. government's funding of HIV-prevention measures)?

Would legislation work for prevention? What is the role of government in terms of prevention, aside from legislation?]

Panel 3: Questions and Answers

[Question: (Marisa Ugarte) Sex tourists come from the U.S. to Costa Rica. Brazilian and Costa Rican governments have made it illegal to engage in prostitution with a minor, and, in their countries, they run public service announcements (PSAs) to convey that message. They have asked U.S. tourism councils to put similar PSAs on airplanes. U.S. agencies responded negatively. What motivates U.S. agencies to do this?

Answer: (Marsha Liss) U.S. airlines have not been receptive, and the government does not have the authority to force the airlines to comply. The airlines are worried that if they publicize the harm of prostitution, people will not fly on their planes. However, there has been a recent development with the Bureau of Immigration and Customs Enforcement in the newly formed Homeland Security Office. Customs officers will be handing out the brochures at the gates of flights to targeted destinations. This brochure will highlight the criminality of prostitution. They are working to get other departments on board with a brochure that would be handed out to American passengers to targeted destinations. Hopefully, as airlines notice that the passengers are not responding negatively to the brochures, then airlines will do the same. It may even infiltrate into travel and tourism agencies. For foreign policy reasons, it is better that the government initiate the program and serve as an example for other governments with the hopes of initiating voluntary private compliance.

Question: (Twiss Butler) Women travel agents have spoken about this issue. Has the American Association of Women Travel Agents gotten involved in targeting aircraft passengers to target countries?

Answer: (Marsha Liss) They are not involved directly. There is a grassroots approach by other organizations, and they are involved through them.

Comment: (Kenneth Franzblau) Efforts should be made to go further. Let travelers know when they go to certain countries that prostitution with a minor is illegal. This warning should be framed as a way to help the traveler not face prosecutions for breaking the law.

Comment: (Sandra Hunnicutt) Captive Daughters worked on a sex tour demonstration, but did work with the American Society of Travel Agents (ASTA) who highly resisted. The travel industry will only comply kicking and screaming because they still want to portray these destinations as marvelous holidays and ignore the reason why many people frequent them. There will be no significant progress unless there are incentives.

Comment: (Marisa Ugarte) There needs to be international protection laws to hold pedophiles who have committed crimes in multiple countries accountable. International extradition laws need to expedite the process of violators to be tried in their countries of origin. Governments should not be scared to prosecute. Something needs to be done to ratify such treaties between countries. We should emphasize in PSA videos on airplanes that it is illegal to engage in prostitution with children. There should be something included in customs information that warns travelers of local laws when they enter the country. In Costa Rica, when people enter the country, there is a sign stating that it is illegal to engage in prostitution with a child. The U.S. needs to put such a sign in the customs areas.

Comment: (Kirsi Ayre) In West Africa, women are compelled to exchange sex for commodities, and many find that because they are not exchanging sex for money it is not prostitution. Organizations must be helped in making people see that "barter" can be prostitution, too. This recognition could help funding, especially because African AIDS efforts are highly funded.

Comment: (Melissa Farley) There are problems with using HIV Prevention as a way to help prostitutes. For example, the Thai government is using the cover of preventing HIV as a justification for the legalization of prostitution. They claim that by regulating prostitution, they will be able to distribute condoms and prevent HIV. Millions of dollars go to HIV-prevention groups that advocate legalization. Giving prostitutes condoms does not prevent HIV. Safe sex negotiations can actually threaten their lives; many can be beaten or killed just for asking. It is up to the customer to use a condom and many refuse. The only way to protect these women from HIV is to stop prostitution.

Comment: (Dorchen Leidholt) Priscilla Alexander (the leader of COYOTE) was hired by a health care agency to develop policies on HIV that are used to promote the acceptance of prostitution as a legitimate form of work. We must look at where the money is going (*i.e.*, to organizations that promote the legalization of prostitution) and who ends up making these key policy decisions.

Comment: (Donna Hughes) The U.S. passed a policy stating that it would not give money to groups that promote legalization, but many such groups are still receiving funds. The World Health Organization (WHO) advocates the legalization of prostitution by claiming that the protection of prostitutes is a way to fight AIDS. WHO is in violation of our current policies, yet it still gets a significant amount of funding from the U.S. (about 40 percent of their budget). Currently, some U.S. and other organizations, such as WHO, are trying to thwart Russia's efforts to pass an important anti-trafficking law. Many organizations are trying to get in the way of this law because they want to pass a law that recognizes prostitution as a legitimate form of work. Duma (Russian Parliament) deputies began to take notice of the people coming to lobby, and they decided that the best way to stop AIDS was to fight prostitution. Sixteen members of Parliament wrote to the U.S. Congress asking them to stop funding these non-governmental organizations that were promoting legalization. They stood up to the U.S. The letter indicates that the new law will give Russia tools to combat its serious problem with trafficking and prostitution by making pimping a major crime. The Duma, however, finds itself under pressure by U.S. organizations that hand out information, pass out condoms, and encourage young women to choose prostitution as a job. This form of "harm reduction" is hurting Russian women. Russia stated that they are trying to restore the moral value of its youth, and the NGOs are undermining these efforts. The U.S. President spoke out against trafficking (in a recent speech at the United Nations); yet, the U.S continues to demoralize Russia. It is hypocritical for the U.S. to condemn trafficking while funding organizations like these. Russians state that "if a policy is not acceptable in America, please to not export it to us." They ask Congress to treat Russian children like America treats its own.

Comment: (Kaethe Morris Hoffer) We should not think of the work against HIV/AIDS as monolithic. It is becoming more feminist. The U.N. has recognized and made clear that increasing the equality of women is a way of stopping the spread of AIDS. There are great allies outside this country in the fight against HIV/AIDS. Harm reduction efforts are also not monolithically in favor of legalization. We will often support the efforts of HIV- and harm-reduction organizations.

Comment: (John Picarelli) There is a need to create mandates to train local law enforcement agencies and show them what they can do. There have been massive changes since 9/11, and organizations formed under Homeland Security are still seeking out their roles. We should convince them that their role should be to fight trafficking. The border patrol does work with smuggling, but not with trafficking. Yes, there should be a global effort, but there also needs to be a local effort fought within the community. We need "glocalization."

Question: (Lisa Thompson) There is a need for state laws to empower local law enforcement. Is anyone working on a model state law? Some have passed, but there have been problems. If there is such a model, is it abolitionist? We should also talk about networks and coalitions and look to the domestic violence movement, which already has connections with local law enforcement, education, funds, and outreach to schools. There is the possibility of combining efforts with the domestic violence movement.

Comment: (Dorchen Leidholt) The domestic violence movement has developed the model for seeing the necessity of protecting the victim and blaming the perpetrator. Those in the movement understand violence against women, and they should understand that prostitution is a form of domestic violence.

Comment: (Kristen Houser) Before the National Organization against Sexual Assault fell apart, there were many divisive arguments between the legalization and abolition folks. There was not across the board support–not everyone "got it." The Violence Against Women Act is coming up for reauthorization in 2005. A change in the Military Code that would have zero-tolerance for engaging in prostitution with a minor is on the tables. This Code would hold that not knowing the age of the prostitute is no longer an excuse. Also, we must push for the adoption of a provision that states that, in order to receive VAWA funds, an organization cannot promote regulation, legalization, or tolerance zones. There are areas in which domestic violence and sexual assault can provide a model for us that has worked, but we need to be careful because many things have not worked. We should learn from their mistakes, use those models and tweak them. We need to transition from crisis intervention to long-term help for survivors of trafficking.

Comment: (Vidya Samarasinghe) There is a lot of funding out there. We need to figure out a better approach it and intervene to make a difference. The National Institute of Health (NIH) has a lot of money for HIV, and it does fund some policy organizations. There is a need to make clear to everyone that prostitution is illegal.

Question: (Melissa Farley) Many have learned that statements coming from the U.N. and the Center for Disease Control (CDC) sound good for equality of women, but find that the Special Rapporteur for violence against women supports the legalization of prostitution. We must look deeper at where is the money going.

Comment: (Derek Ellerman) A state model law has been developed with a protection policy that is abolitionist. It will be released soon.

Question: (Ruth Pojman) Different uses of terms cause a lot of confusion. We should think about how language should be used. There are different forms of harm reduction. Should there be different terms used to describe the various tactics? For example, we should look at the implications of the term "cross generational sex relations."

Answer: (Donna Hughes) The term "cross generational sex relations" comes straight out of pedophile literature. It is appalling that the U.S. government is providing funding in sub-Saharan Africa to prevent the spread of AIDS in "cross generational sex relations." The government is actually endorsing and facilitating statutory rape and child abuse. For example, one program brought high-school girls together to discuss how they could convince their "sugar daddyies" to wear condoms. This approach is not getting to the root of the problem and, instead, is maintaining the perpetuation of violence against young girls. The language of "harm reduction" has evolved. Harm reduction grew out of efforts to reduce drug use, and the pro-legalization camp adopted its tactics. The term has grown, but it does not mean the same thing to everyone. Those who want a tolerant approach to prostitution know that it will not be popular, so they (e.g., groups like COYOTE) have developed code terms to hide underneath. We always have to be alert to what the new code terms are and the labels they are operating under in order to get funds.

Comment: (Kirsi Ayre) Some of these organizations in sub-Saharan Africa are promoting the use of female condoms as a method of "feminist empowerment"–a choice the woman makes because the man does not agree. There are advertisements on TV advocating this in Africa.

Comment: (Dorchen Leidholt) There is an intersection of domestic violence and trafficking with the internet bride industry. There is a need to develop federal legislation for this industry.

Comment: (Kenneth Franzblau) The mail-order bride industry is just the other side of the trafficking/ sex tourism coin. Mail-order brides do not have the opportunity to protect themselves any more than trafficking victims do. Federal legislation is toughening up by drafting immigration policies that require greater disclosure by the male sponsor (criminal record, medical past, any orders of protection, etc.). By the time the women got the information they needed about the men, they were already too far into the process. If women know more information, then it gives them the ability to act. The information must be provided in the native language of the potential fiancée. A great deal of paperwork may make it more difficult for men to operate. Many mail-order bride companies will now have to meet regulations. If the legislation goes through, it will make it harder to manipulate a woman to come to the U.S. as a bride.

Comment: (Vidya Samarasinghe) In order for the legislation to be effective, there is a need for harmonization of the laws. Women receive vital information about their future husbands very late in the process because there is not harmonization of international law. By the time these women receive the information, they can rationalize anything because they are extremely enticed by the "pot of gold." Laws in the U.S. alone would not help without harmonization.

Comment: (Ruth Pojman) In some cases, mail-order bride agencies are just fronts for sex tourism. Women would think that men are coming to see if they want them for their wives. The men would visit, they would not bring any gifts, they would have sex with her, and leave. There was no intention to marry her; it was just sex tourism. There are licensed travel agencies, but many are actually trafficking agencies that the authorities have not investigated. In Moscow, there is a "Pretty Woman" syndrome because of the glamorization of the sex industry. This can be countered by doing more media work to counter mass media's glamorization of prostitution.

Comment: (Kristen Houser) Many victims of domestic violence and sexual assault on the national level know that they have been photographed or videotaped. We need to try to get domestic violence shelters to document these issues. If we could screen victims and ask about being photographed, filmed, pimped, and swapped, this would provide information to support our claims that violence against women is interconnected and the perpetrators are often involved in multiple forms of female exploitation.

Comment: (Sandra Hunnicutt) A woman in the Philippines inquired about a job opportunity that she was offered in California. After investigation, the firm did not exist. A solution to this problem is to create a website that lists the registered corporations and agencies in each state. If the firm is not listed, the woman should not come. If the firm is listed but is a front, it can then be prosecuted for false advertising.

Comment: (Marisa Ugarte) The U.S. needs to take responsibility for being a recipient country. Land and sea entry points need regulation, not just the airports.

Comment: (Meredith McGowan) We must ask survivors of domestic violence what their perpetrators are doing to other women. Many abuse a lot of other women before they bring it home to their wife and kids.

Comment: (Donna Hughes) Lobbying with coalitions for domestic violence and sexual assault will be beneficial. We need people from those coalitions to start speaking up and to start talking to their constituency (Democrats). Abolition should not be a conservative Republican issue, even though the Republicans have passed all of the favorable legislation thus far. The Democrats are trying to undermine anti-legalization by granting money to organizations that promote tolerance. When the sex trafficking act was passed, Paul Wellstone was the only democrat to support it. Democrats must begin to see anti-legalization as their issue, too.

Comment: (Dorchen Leidholdt) There are serial sexual predators. In one case, an abuser/exploiter, a swinger involved with por`nography, battered his much younger wife, got custody of the children, and then looked for an Internet bride. He brought a woman back from Russia. Her daughter called the police on him. He would look for global women in order to get the most vulnerable victim. He ended up back on the Internet to get a new Russian bride. He got an internet bride from Belarus. He was drugging and sodomizing her. He was then prosecuted for rape. He was trying to bring over yet another woman from Eastern Europe at the time. He was convicted, and he fled to Poland. We need to get these guys. They go on and prey on more and more vulnerable victims. People have track records that are given little attention.

Comment: (Twiss Butler) We must also pay attention to the track records of pornographers. We have data on 800 women, men, and transgenders in nine countries on the use of pornography. Donna Hughes has a chapter in our new book on online prostitution. There are public assistance monies for women willing to get out of prostitution.

Comment: (Karin Brandenburg) It is important to note the watershed achievement of the U.N. Trafficking Protocol that will come into effect this year. Governments will be required to report on their compliance with the trafficking mechanism. The American Bar Association created an assessment mechanism that can be adapted to investigate each country's compliance with the new protocol. Each country will submit its own report, but the universal assessment mechanism can be used to check the accuracy and legitimacy of each country's findings. These "shadow reports" can be used against governments in violation of the protocols.

Question: (Ruth Pojman) What rights does a woman have if her husband is abusing her and she does not have a green card?

Comment: (Dorchen Leidholdt) The Violence Against Women Act has clauses for protecting women, such as mail-order brides. VAWA 2000 provides a new remedy under the U-Visa. U-Visas are for victims of gender-motivated crimes that help to prosecute violators. In return, she will receive help in acquiring residency and work authorization. It is now possible to submit U-Visa certification to the INS, which will issue deferred action status.

Answer: (Marsha Liss) T-Visas are another tool that women can utilize for protection. They were developed to offer much broader services to a wider range of women. The government has authorized the use of 5,000 T-Visas, but only 400 were issued last year because there were very few referrals for the service. There may be reluctance among those women in turning to local law officials. Non-governmental organizations need to facilitate dialogue among women in order that they can trust this tool. Federal prosecutors find these cases too difficult to deal with. Advocates can help prosecutors understand the cumbersome laws.

Comment: (Dorchen Leidholt) Through deferred action status, women can be in the U.S. legally. They can also receive work authorization and health benefits. The Center for Battered Women's Legal Services has created model certification forms for U-Visas.]

Panel 4:
What Can Be Done to Interfere with and Ultimately Eliminate Demand?

Moderator: Norma Hotaling

The Abuse, Rape, and Trafficking of Children and Adults through Prostitution Will End by Eliminating the Demand and Focusing on Protection[1]

What we call "child prostitution" needs to be clearly, strongly, and unambiguously defined as sexual abuse on young human beings. This sexual abuse of children through prostitution is made possible by a society that has created, sanctioned, and institutionalized numbers of children for whom routine abuse, torture, rape, and kidnapping is considered acceptable. The legal, mental, and medical health and human rights consequences of this abuse remains with the child as he or she is arrested, prosecuted, jailed, placed on probation, and forced into treatment. In essence, what we are saying and enforcing through laws and inappropriate interventions is that children and youth are consenting to their own sexual abuse and that by consenting to this abuse they are a danger to society. They are subject to arrest; they are viewed as perpetrators, not victims; and they are denied any services for their victimization. I believe that we can end child prostitution by renaming and redefining it as child abuse and statutory rape.

In the *Lancet Medical Journal* of May 2002, Dr. Barry Levy of Tufts University School of Medicine in Boston states, "The prostitution of children and related health consequences has been accepted for too long. The time has come to make them unacceptable." The use and trafficking of children and adolescents in the sex industry is widespread around the world and the U.S. is no exception. An estimated 10 million children worldwide are already involved in the $20 billion-a-year sex industry, and this number is increasing by about one million each year. Richard J. Estes, a University of Pennsylvania professor of social work and the author of *The Commercial Sexual Exploitation of Children in the U.S., Canada and Mexico* (2001), says, "Child sexual exploitation is the most hidden form of child abuse in the U.S. and North America today. It is the nation's least recognized epidemic." According to his report, there are between 200,000 and 300,000 U.S. children involved in the sex trade and/or trafficked into prostitution. While the exact number is impossible to calculate, all experts agree it is an epidemic and, clearly, the numbers are rising.

In keeping with the international figures, prostituted children in the U.S. face an increased risk of: sexual and physical assault; suicide; pregnancy; abortion; sexually transmitted diseases, including AIDS; post-traumatic stress disorder; and death. Statistics reveal that 75-95 percent of all thirteen to eighteen-year-old girls in our justice system have been victims of abuse. Many of these girls have been exploited for pornography or have suffered or witnessed physical and sexual violence. For these girls, the average age of entry into prostitution is thirteen to fourteen years old. At this critical point in their development, these girls are introduced to what becomes for most, an endless cycle of arrest, drug addiction, and violence. The results, as one might imagine, are traumatic and lead to a host of disempowered behaviors, including dropping out of school, prostitution, addiction, selling drugs, and violence. Their exploitation is perpetuated by a continued reliance on the very people who have physically, emotionally, and sexually assaulted them. These children come from all racial, ethnic and socioeconomic groups, though a preponderance of them come from the least advantaged, isolated, and disorganized segments. As a result of abuse and neglect, they have lost the support and guidance that a healthy family and environment provide. As these children move into adulthood, their situations remain unrecognized and untreated, and they continue a downward spiral of drugs, re-victimization, institutionalization, and death.

Pimps and traffickers are responding to the increased profitability spurred by increased demand. Everyday, in densely populated urban areas, girls of color aged ten to seventeen are lured from local high schools by violent pimps. Poor and vulnerable Asian, South American, Central American, and Russian women and girls are smuggled, kidnapped, raped, tricked, and coerced by traffickers and organized-crime syndicates into the highly invisible and mobile sex trade that includes strip clubs, escort services, massage parlors, brothels, and street prostitution. A steady *supply* of vulnerable and naive thirteen- and fourteen-year-old blond, blue-eyed girls are brutally and cunningly recruited from schools, streets, shopping malls, and online chat rooms in the Midwest and Canada to fill the *demand* side of sexual exploitation: comprised mostly by educated, middle- and upper-class men.

Though existing laws indicate that they should be charged with sexual abuse and statutory rape, police rarely if ever investigate, arrest, or prosecute "johns." At most, the police cite men as users of adult prostitutes. If a girl admits she is underage or if the police know, she is taken to jail. Men are released. They are often told, "this is your lucky day," or "go on home, buddy, we don't want to ruin your life," never once thinking of the life of the child that is ruined and changed forever or of a young mind and body so brutally traumatized over and over. We can end child prostitution, but it will not happen until we focus on the sexual abusers of children–the "johns." We also must do more than just talk about pimps, traffickers, and their complex organizations, well-funded networks, and brutal manipulative tactics. We can end child prostitution when we completely reorganize our definitions and when we create major changes in how we respond.

Traditionally, our social response to child sexual abuse has been either complete denial or blaming the child. We have documented instances of U.S. judges describing five year-old children as "provocative" or "promiscuous," and our legal system has a long history of shaming girls and boys who are the targets of adult sexual violence. For most of our social and legal history, being sexually assaulted or violated meant that the victim, whether child or adult, acquired the status of "whore"–someone who is, supposedly, without credibility, rights, or respect. We have begun to shift our relationship to children, to adult women, and to sexual violence. Policy makers, law enforcement officials, and the general public are beginning to come to the understanding that rape is truly a crime–not solely in legal terms–but a crime against the human rights of the victim and against all human beings who want to live in a safe and healthy society.

Our shifting beliefs have been mirrored in practice: it is a crime for an adult to have sex with a child; it is a crime to have sex without consent. The perpetrators of these crimes can at least hypothetically be arrested, prosecuted, and incarcerated. The victims of these crimes, at least hypothetically, are entitled to justice, victim's compensation, and protection. We have begun to challenge the idea that a person's appearance, dress, or social status define whether or not she or he can truly be recognized as a victim, or the idea that some people are "deserving" victims.

When it comes to prostitution however, in ideology and practice, it's as if no changes have occurred. As long as someone is labeled a prostitute–whether child or adult, we still say that it is OK to dehumanize, to mistreat, and to endanger that person. The children we call "prostitutes" are in reality the children who we have designated as acceptable and blame-worthy targets for sexual abuse. There is no law that states a child can consent to sexual abuse, and by doing so be arrested. But still we arrest children and deny them services. Unfortunately, there are several ways in which we have created a group of kids who it's okay to sexually abuse:

We ignore the abuse. We are misdefining sexually abused children as criminals perpetrating a crime, rather than as victims of crime. When a child tells a court-mandated reporter or police officer that they have had sex with an adult and received money, that reporter or officer is, and should be, legally bound to report the incident as an instance of child sexual abuse. Not only does this reporting not occur, the child is at risk of criminalization and punishment.

We encourage the perpetrators. By focusing on the behavior or supposed wrongs of children, we are ignoring the perpetrators. We rarely go after the pimps, and almost never go after the "johns," and thus, never arrest the men as sexual abusers. Even calling them "johns," rather than child sexual abusers, helps misrepresent what's happening and creates an acceptable group of children to abuse. As a society, we are encouraging and enabling the perpetrators of child sexual abuse; we are creating a group of men who are learning–through adult prostitution–how to be sex abusers of children and often how to be torturers and batterers. Many of these men bring these behaviors home or into other social arenas, and most of them continue to prey on children within the sex industries.

We don't connect adult users of prostitutes and the sexual abuse of children through prostitution. Studies show that most prostituted children tend to be concentrated in the cheaper end of the prostitution market, where conditions are the worst and the concentration of customers the highest. Although some children are prostituted by and/or specifically for pedophiles and preferential abusers, the majority *of the several million men who annually exploit prostitutes under the age of eighteen are first and foremost prostitute users who become child sexual abusers through their prostitute use, rather than the other way around.* The world of prostitution, whether legal or illegal, provides an arena where laws and rules that constrain sex with minors can be evaded. Laws and social conventions make it difficult and dangerous for individuals to buy children for sexual purposes in non-commercial contexts, but prostitution potentially provides instant access, often to a selection of children. When asked how a person justifies having sex with an underage prostituted child, men surveyed in the First Offenders Prostitution Program respond, "they don't even think." They know that law enforcement efforts are focused on the youth/child and not on them. Prevention programs should offer the stern message: age is not a defense. You will be prosecuted, jailed, and required to register as a sex offender after your release from prison. In short, the message should be, "Your life will be over, and your next victim will be spared." After working with over 6,000 men/johns, I have found that they feel they have a lot to lose and will change their behavior when given the correct message backed by severe consequences.

We don't give kids a way out. Our approach to the sexual abuse of children within prostitution rarely involves the creation of resources that truly enable healing and recovery, rather than punishment and stigma. The Office of Victim Compensation and other resources intended to meet the needs of crime victims deny resources to children abused through child prostitution, based on the misdefinition of these children as criminals. This means that resources are rarely available in any venue that does not involve the humiliation and vulnerability of arrest and incarceration. If the child is arrested, she or he is cycled through the criminal justice system, sometimes repeatedly, intensifying the shame, pain, and vulnerability that make children easy prey to pimps and abusers, and decreasing the possibility of successful intervention.

We are working in "crisis mode" rather than on prevention. Arresting children or even arresting traffickers or pimps is a very far cry from preventing the problem. Rather than responding to the urgent needs of children who are being abused, we are still asking them to prove to us that they are not one of the "bad kids." We must communally reject the myth that if a girl is on the street wearing lipstick and a miniskirt she can somehow consent to sexual abuse and that by consenting, she has committed a crime. When a child sexual abuser says, "but she said she was 18," we must realize that this is not a defense against child sexual abuse or statutory rape. This message must be accompanied by a strong public education campaign and rehabilitation options, or these men will simply seek new victims or take the abusive behaviors home. While it is important to address crises among abused youth, the long-term eradication of the problem will be achieved only by establishing prevention programs for boys, men, and girls, and full criminal sanctions focused on the abusers, buyers, pimps, and traffickers.

The following are key components to the systemic change that must occur to successfully address child prostitution:

Define the issue. Court-mandated reporters, such as law enforcement personnel, probation officers, judges, and lawyers, must be educated and required to correctly define and report child prostitution as child sexual abuse, to define the so-called prostitutes as abused children, and to define the so-called johns as child sexual abusers. Mandated reporters must have a

94

clear understanding of what, when, and how they are required to report sexual abuse and that to not report abuse is illegal. After receiving training, the mandated reporters must be held accountable.

Educate the Public in order to better recognize child sexual abuse in and out of prostitution. We must recognize the clear links between child and adult prostitution on a global scale and not presume that anyone labeled a prostitute is responsible for a system in which we allow people to buy human bodies. Only by transforming our relationships to all forms of sexual exploitation and abuse, whether of child or adult, can we disempower a multibillion-dollar sex industry in which the average age of entry is thirteen to fourteen and a society in which many adult men are socialized, from boyhood, to feel entitled to sexual service.

Reform legislative practice. We must utilize our existing laws, as well as child abuse prevention and treatment resources. There needs to be a mechanism to move a child from the juvenile system into the family courts. It is time to redefine child prostitution within its correct legislative framework: child safety. We need dramatic legislative reform, requiring total decriminalization of children and increased prosecution of pimps and the people actually creating the demand for child sexual abuse and making it profitable: the customers. Adults who sexually abuse children in prostitution must face prosecution and consequences already afforded by our child protection laws, including becoming registered sex offenders.

Build coalitions and provide training. U.S. federal laws, such as the Mann Act and the Protection of Children from Sexual Predators Act, are intended to address the issue of interstate trafficking in children for prostitution and pornography. However, though laws exist, they are not being actively enforced. Existing state laws regarding the use of children for sexual purposes vary in content and in the penalties imposed on offenders. Enforcement and coordination among local, state, and federal law enforcement officials are sporadic at best. Furthermore, many child and youth-service public and private agencies do not have policies, procedures, or resources in place to serve victims of commercial sexual exploitation and are often unaware of federal laws or how to access the support of federal agencies. The results are either that children and youth are apprehended and treated as offenders/perpetrators and entered into the justice system where services typically do not exist or are not available to them or they are redirected to service agencies not prepared to provide the comprehensive treatment necessary to address the trauma and need for healing surrounding sexual exploitation.

Create a real escape for children through social services and recovery. A web of services, which responds to the torture, kidnap, and extremes of violence that characterize pimping, pandering and trafficking, absolutely must accompany legislative change. Without a safety net and resource base, taking children out of the criminal justice system only means returning them to pimps and perpetrators. Don't use protection and safety as an excuse to build more and better services for youth in detention. Be focused, vigilant, and logical in our approach.

Direct victims-of-violent-crimes resources toward rehabilitating these children. When victims of violent crimes are not referred to the appropriate social services, we are clearly saying that these children and youth are consenting to their own sexual and physical abuse and that is a crime for which they should be punished and denied services.

Focus on prevention. We need sustained attention to all the social causes of prostitution, including but not limited to: gaping problems in our social response to child abuse within families and communities; extremes of poverty; outdated legal doctrines and practices; gender inequality; racial stratification; and a horrifying view that prostituted children have no value or rights.

I founded SAGE because fourteen years ago. I was exiting the criminal justice system. I was in juvenile halls, jails, psychiatric hospitals, emergency rooms, and drug treatment programs since I was twelve. No one ever asked me about my life, about prostitution, about being beaten, raped, or kidnapped. I was just a whore, a dope fiend, and a criminal. How could I get out? No one ever treated me like a person. No one asked me if I hurt or why.

Like 90 percent of our clients, I experienced sexual abuse, including child prostitution. Like 82 percent of our clients, I had been brutally assaulted, and like 84 percent of us, I had been homeless. Like most of my clients, I suffered severe symptoms of PTSD; and I desperately wanted to get out of prostitution and a life that made no sense to me. Many girls like myself, if untreated, cycle endlessly through medical, mental, social services, and criminal justice systems as high users, costing cities billions of dollars annually.

As a survivor-advocate turned service provider, I am often expected by my colleagues in government to endorse or participate in finding new ways to criminalize or increase the incarceration time of children, supposedly in the name of protection. My sense of ethics, my experiential understanding of the issues, and my respect for the lives of children and all human beings requires that I reject the idea that people who are abused are *de facto* criminals.

All children deserve to be humanized and to be free of sexual exploitation. The crime we need to confront and immediately redress is the betrayal and scapegoating of the most vulnerable members of our society–by some of the most powerful institutions of our society. When we do this, we will end child prostitution. We can end child prostitution today by naming it what it really is: the most severe form of child abuse.

Panelist: Mohammed Y. Mattar

Thank you for inviting me to participate in this important conference about the very important issue of the demand in sex trafficking.

I am here to speak on one aspect of the problem of demand and that is the appropriate legal response to sex trafficking.

I think it is appropriate to start with the international legal response to the problem of demand, since only a few days ago the

United Nations Protocol to Prevent, Suppress and Punish Trafficking in Persons, Especially Women and Children, became law. Article 17(4) of the Protocol ("instruments of ratification") has been satisfied, and hence the Protocol is in force, now that 42 countries have ratified. Denmark was the last to ratify on September 30th [2003], and on September 26th [2003] Belize, Laos, Poland, and Rwanda ratified the Protocol.

Article 9(5) of the Protocol addresses the issue of demand as an issue of prevention, stating that:

> States Parties shall adopt or strengthen legislative or other measures, such as educational, social or cultural measures, including through bilateral and multilateral cooperation, to discourage the demand that fosters of exploitation of persons, especially women and children, that leads to trafficking.

Thus, the Protocol talks about legislative, educational, social, and cultural measures, and makes the link between demand and trafficking.

Let me talk about some of the legislative measures that countries may take to discourage the demand. Some legal systems do not go after the customer. Prostitution in these countries is legal. The act of prostitution itself is acceptable. Only prostitution-related activities constitute a crime, and if the act of prostitution does not constitute a crime, why punish the customer who is obtaining a service, which is legal in nature? Sex in consideration for money is permissible.

Other legal systems penalize both the women in prostitution and the customer. That is the Islamic law approach in Muslim countries such as Saudi Arabia, Iran, Pakistan, Yemen, Mauritania, Jordan, Bahrain, Sudan, Tunisia, Malaysia, Brunei, and the United Arab Emirates, where the customer who buys sexual service from a woman in prostitution is considered to be committing adultery–a crime under Islamic law which punishes both the adulterer and the adulteress.

A third approach is taken by Sweden–the January 1, 1999, law that makes buying casual sexual services a crime, the Swedish Act, provides that "a person who obtains casual sexual relations in exchange for payment shall be sentenced–unless the act is punishable under the Swedish Penal Code–for the purchase of sexual services to a fine or imprisonment for at most six months." Buying sex is a crime, but selling sex is not. Under this new law, the data for 1999 indicates that ninety-four cases were reported, with ten resulting in conviction; in 2000, there were ninety-two cases prosecuted under this law, resulting in twenty-nine convictions; and, in 2001, eighty-six prosecutions resulted in thirty-eight convictions.

In few legal systems, knowledge of trafficking makes the customer liable. This approach is adopted by Art. 41-A of the Criminal Code of Macedonia, which provides that anyone that uses or enables another person's usage of sexual service from the person for whom he knows are victims of human trafficking will be punished with six months and up to five years imprisonment. The new legislation of Croatia (May 2003) follows the Macedonian model in criminalizing the act to the customer if he has knowledge that the person in prostitution has been trafficked.

When the customer is a tourist engaging in sex with a child, child sex-tourism must be recognized as a crime. And the Protect Act which was signed by President Bush this past April [2003] and to which he made reference in his latest speech to the United Nations, prohibits United States citizens and residents from traveling abroad to engage in illicit sexual activity with a child. The Protect Act makes the proof of the crime easier. It is no longer required to prove intent to have sex with a child abroad.

On the day following President Bush's speech, Michael Lewis Clark, a sixty-nine-year-old retired U.S. Army sergeant, was charged with sex tourism in one of the first indictments under the new law. Clark was indicted by a Seattle grand jury on two counts of traveling via foreign commerce to Cambodia to engage in illicit sexual conduct with a minor. He paid two young, homeless boys, aged ten and thirteen, $2 each to have sex with him. Working with two NGOs to gain a prosecution of Clark, Cambodian and U.S. Customs officials will bring witnesses from Cambodia to the United States if the case goes to trial. Clark is unlikely to be offered a deal as the U.S. Attorney General, John Ashcroft, has discouraged plea-bargaining throughout the country.

When the customer is associated with the U.S. military, a different approach must be taken. According to the Military Extraterritorial Jurisdiction Act of 2000, criminal jurisdiction is established for "acts committed by persons employed by or accompanying military forces outside the United States, including civilian employees of the Department of Defense and its contractors, if such acts would carry prison sentences of over one year within the United States." This is an extraterritorial application of the law, but you have a problem when you have peacekeeping.

There are currently thirteen U.N.-peacekeeping missions operating around the world. Rule 4 of the U.N. General Assembly Code of Conduct of 1993 says that U.N. peacekeepers should "not indulge in immoral acts of sexual, physical or psychological abuse or exploitation of the local population or United Nations staff, especially women and children." However, in the case of Bosnia, the demand for prostitution has risen significantly with the arrival of U.N. peacekeepers. Until the mid-1990s, the sex-slave industry barely existed in Bosnia, but after the signing of the Dayton Accord in 1995 and with the arrival of approximately 50,000 male peacekeepers, a sex-trade market has been created. Women from Belarus, Moldova, Ukraine, Romania, Hungary, and Albania have been lured to Bosnia by offers of legal work, but instead are enslaved in brothels. U.N. peacekeepers are under the exclusive criminal jurisdiction of their own national authorities and have immunity from local prosecution. It is up to the U.N. Board of Inquiry to find reasonable grounds for a charge of serious misconduct with a recommendation that the peacekeeper be repatriated for subsequent disciplinary action in his native country. Of only twenty-four officers repatriated to their countries for misconduct, none have been prosecuted for violating Rule 4 of the U.N. General Assembly Code of Conduct.

When the customer is looking for a bride, this is non-commercial sex. In the event that non-commercial sex involves abuse, it should be considered an illicit activity, especially in cases of forced marriages, arranged marriages, early marriages, temporary marriages, marriages for the purpose of childbearing, and mail-order brides. Mail-order brides may be classified as trafficking for the purpose of labor or a case of sex trafficking. Section 652 of the United States Illegal Immigration Reform and Immigrant Responsibility Act of 1996 imposes upon the matchmaking organizations an obligation to inform the prospective bride:

> upon recruitment, such immigration and naturalization information as the Immigration and Naturalization Service deems appropriate, in the recruit's native language, including information regarding conditional permanent residence status and the battered spouse waiver under such status, permanent resident status, marriage fraud penalties, the unregulated nature of

the business engaged in by such organizations, and the study required under subsection (c).

But this is not enough. Matchmaking organizations should be criminally liable for illicit activities related to trafficking, and the customer who abuses his bride must also be punished. The Internet provides an additional source for demand in the sex industry. It has become a tool to aid international sex syndicates, who deceive women from different countries and who are then enslaved.

The Internet may also be used by sex "tourists." Foreigners may make arrangements from their homes to engage in prostitution after they arrive in countries such as Thailand. Internet sites offer to help men find a bride in exchange for cash.

Airlines should become involved in the campaign to educate sex tourists through the use of education information broadcast during flights to countries where sex tourism has become popularized. The TVPA, although it does not explicitly cover sex tourism, makes the point, in Section 105 (d) (5), that one of the main tasks of the Interagency Task Force to Monitor and Combat Trafficking is to: "Examine the role of the international 'sex tourism' industry in the trafficking of persons and in the sexual exploitation of women and children around the world." However, the new amendment to the TVP A, under H.R. 2620, provides that:

(e) COMBATING INTERNATIONAL SEX TOURISM- (1) DEVELOPMENT AND DISSEMINATION OF MATERI-ALS- The President, pursuant to such regulations as may be prescribed, shall (A) require that airlines organized under the laws of the United States and other airlines operating in the United States develop and disseminate materials alerting travelers that sex tourism (as defined in section 2423 (c-e) of title 18, United States Code) is illegal, will be prosecuted, and presents dangers to those involved, and (B) encourage such airlines to work with nongovernmental organizations in developing these materials. Such materials may include, for example, brochures, public service announcements, and billboards.

Unfortunately, the 2003 TIP Report does not consider the issue of demand.

As I stated in my testimony before the House Committee on International Relations on June 25, 2003, the TIP Report addresses the issue of demand by making explicit references to the law of Sweden stating that "the Government...passed a pioneering law that criminalizes the purchase rather than the sale of sex..." The TIP Report also makes reference to the Islamic law approach to the issue of demand, explicitly stating that in Saudi Arabia "Islamic law prohibits sexual relationships outside the context of marriage and provides for strict penalties if the law is breeched." The TIP Report rightly criticizes the application of Islamic law in Pakistan when it states "[i]f rape or forced prostitution cases are prosecuted under the Islamic law-oriented Hudood ordinances, victims are reluctant to testify since the woman's testimony is tantamount to an admission of adultery if prosecutors conclude that her testimony does not meet the burden of proof." This application is inconsistent with Qur'anic legislation, which states that women should not be forced into prostitution, and, if they are compelled, they should not be punished because they have been forced into prostitution.[2]

In a statement I submitted for a hearing before the Committee on International Relations, House of Representatives, 107th Congress, Second Session, June 19, 2002, I stated that the TVPA does not require that the TIP Report takes into consideration "the extent of trafficking," but only "the extent to which the country is a country of origin, transit, or destination for severe forms of trafficking." Warning about the harm of prostitution must be addressed in any program that warns against the danger of trafficking.

It is not clear to what extent the 2003 TIP Report takes into consideration the issue of demand in placing countries in certain tiers. Only the countries of Ghana, Lithuania, Morocco, and the United Arab Emirates, out of the twenty-six countries placed on Tier 1, outlaw prostitution. The other twenty-two countries legalize, decriminalize, or tolerate prostitution. This approach is inconsistent with the TVPA, which explicitly distinguishes between sex trafficking and labor trafficking and does not consider sex as a form of labor. A review of this approach is imperative in light of the Trafficking in Persons National Security Directive of February 2003, which explicitly states that "[p]rostitution

---

[2] Holy Qu'ran, Surah 24:33

and related activities, which are inherently harmful and dehumanizing, contribute to the phenomenon of trafficking in persons."

What does this mean?

1. Prostitution must be defined as a "commercial sex act" but not as "commercial sex work."

2. It is not enough that the law considers illegal the behavior of the customer of sexual services. The behavior of the customer who obtains sexual services, the functional equivalent of the law must also recognize such behavior as unacceptable. By "functional equivalent of the law," I mean the traditions, the customs, the acceptable behavior of the people. The legal systems that "tolerate" or "accommodate" or "normalize" the behavior of the customer must reconsider its policies, change the law, and enforce the law accordingly.

3. The liability of the legal person, as opposed to the national person, must be established. It is not enough to go after the customer. We have to do something about the advertisement agency on the Internet that advertises sex for sale. We also have to address the issue of mail-order brides as a trafficking issue and go after matchmaking organizations. We also have to maximize our legal approach to stripping, massage parlors, escort services, and the like. It is not enough to follow the tort-nuisance approach. We should make these operators of entertainment sex liable for involvement in trafficking, whether for sex or labor. But we have to be careful not to define any of these activities as labor. Again, sex for sale and entertainment-sex should not be defined as labor. There is a moral nuisance issue, which must be addressed, but there is also a criminal liability issue.

Panelist: Pamela Shifman[3]

[Pamela Shifman discussed the sexual violence in Eastern Congo. She stated that, although it was not in the news or on television, it was the largest humanitarian crises in the world, with rape being used as a weapon of war throughout the country. An estimated three million people have been killed. Rape is being used to deliberately and systematically demoralize and victimize women. Women walk for days to reach the nearest hospital for help. There are not even enough beds for

---

[3] Bracketed comments summarized by Sara Dubin and Carolina Chang.

the women who are repeatedly gang-raped. In one hospital, 27 percent of sexual assault survivors are HIV-positive.

Ms. Shifman emphasized the need for social integration among victims. Victims want their families to take them back despite the stigmas and be accepted in their communities, rather than blamed. Women want to feel whole. Husbands will not take their wives back, and daughters are not regarded as worth being taken home. Many women end up on the streets after being raped, since they cannot go home. Many must turn to prostitution for survival.

There is local demand for prostitution; thirty cents could purchase sex. But this humanitarian conflict breeds a larger problem. This problem involves the "big white cars" that appear wherever there is a devastating conflict, namely, the peacekeepers and humanitarian workers. In Eastern Congo, like other places, the demand for prostitution, including child prostitution, increases during conflict. When peacekeepers arrived in Bosnia and Kosovo, demand for prostitution was created that had previously not existed.

In February of 2002, a report was leaked to the media highlighting the sexual exploitation and sexual abuse of children by humanitarian aid workers and peacekeepers in refugee camps in Guinea, Sierra Leone and Liberia. UNHCR and Save the Children interviewed children about their experiences of violence. The interviews revealed that much of the violence that children experienced came from peacekeepers and aid workers. These workers required sex in exchange for basic needs such as blankets and food. These aid workers also traded sex for bubblegum or other items that girls might like. Because of the media attention this report received, the NGOs and U.N. jumped in to try and address this problem. A humanitarian committee (the Interagency Task Force on Protection from Sexual Abuse and Sexual Exploitation in Humanitarian Crises) came together to develop minimum standards for humanitarian workers. The code of conduct forbids any exploitative or manipulative behavior in exchange for aid, and it prohibits sex with a child.

In addition to the new regulations, humanitarian aid workers must change their individual attitudes. Many feel that sex with children is culturally permissible because the children are presumed to be sexually mature. These beliefs can be challenged by discussing the reality of sexual exploitation. Exploitation must be given a human face—we must discuss who these children are and what they have endured. We must also change the institutional structure that allows this behavior to occur with impunity. People need to feel safe to report instances of sexual exploitation. The cultural norms of humanitarian communities must be changed so that people will protect women and children without the risk of losing their jobs.

In the humanitarian community, the code of conduct was passed because of how the story was told: girls were trading sex for survival. This is no different than prostitution. Prostitution is also sex for survival. It is obvious that men in "big trucks" with "big guns" should not exploit refugee girls. The story about prostituted girls in Chicago or Goma or New York is no different. The exploitation of refugee girls is not different from the exploitation of girls and women that takes place in the streets of Chicago or New York or elsewhere. A positive lesson is that if we give victims of exploitation a human face, we can get rules and prohibitions that can help curb exploitation.]

Panelist: Meg Baldwin

Three major themes have stood out for me in our discussion so far in this conference: the *anonymity* of johns, the lack of *accountability* for their behavior and its consequences, and the attribution of *culpability* (by which I mean eligibility for punishment) to women and girls who are prostituted. These conditions are also legally enforced or tolerated. Law enforcement preserves johns' anonymity and their lack of accountability by failing to charge johns with criminal violations for which they are culpable, from solicitation to rape–even murder or its attempt. Few avenues of redress exist outside the criminal justice system for revealing who johns are, or for making them legally accountable for their actions. On the other hand, the culpability of women is reinforced daily in at least two ways: most blatantly, women are consistently targeted for criminal penalties for prostitution. More insidiously, women are allocated all responsibility for the negative effects of prostitution, both to themselves and to others. Under this regime of permissions and punishments, it can come as no surprise that the demand for prostitution flourishes unabated.

In my remarks to follow, I examine three legal arenas in which these themes are played out. The first is in the context of the defense of prostituted women charged with homicide offenses against johns and pimps–a tragic form of self-help intervention on demand. The second is the context of civil restitution claims that may be available to prostituted women against johns. The third is the context of criminal prosecution against johns. I explore how the issues of anonymity, accountability, and culpability are arranged in each of these contexts, and make some recommendations for shifting these patterns in ways that might contribute to decreasing the demand for prostitution.

1. *Self-defense interventions.* The "demand intervention" with which I am most familiar in my work with incarcerated survivors is, sadly, homicide. The first case with which I had significant involvement was that of Aileen Wournos, who was executed by the State of Florida on October 9, 2002–just about one year ago. Ms. Wournos had been arrested and charged with the murder of seven johns over a period of about a year. Other cases came to me through investigation with the Florida Battered Women's Clemency Project, which reviewed murder convictions of nearly two hundred women for killing abusers. One woman killed a man who pimped her, who had come into her life as a john; another woman killed a john whom she had married and later divorced; another woman killed a pimp; two women killed abusive partners after some years in prostitution. All of these women were convicted of serious homicide charges from manslaughter to capital murder.

What were the circumstances of these homicides? In some of these cases, the confrontation with the john appears to have fit the "classic" self-defense pattern. The john posed an immediate threat of deadly force–as traditionally legally understood–and the woman used the same measure of force in resistance. So, in a number of cases, the john threatened a violent rape or advanced on the woman with a weapon; these are the kinds of threats that the law recognizes as justifying the use of deadly force in response. In others, the woman was facing a john whose behavior did not apparently pose a threat of deadly force, at least to a person unfamiliar with the dynamics of prostitution. To the woman, however, the behavior was associated with highly elevated safety and lethality risks when presented by johns, and she responded proportionally to the threat as she saw it. So, in one case, the woman had learned that when a john became angry, called her a "cunt," and insisted on anal sex, she would be lucky to make it out of the encounter alive. During the confrontation that led to the homicide, the john had displayed exactly those behaviors. Finally, in each of the cases that I have explored with the women who committed these acts, they had reached a point of overwhelming distress, the cumulative effects of the abuse they had suffered from so many people for so long a time. All of the impacts of post-traumatic stress disorders had become nearly unendurable for these women–the hyperarousal, intrusive re-experiencing of trauma, the depression and anxiety, impulsive feelings and rage, the suicidal yearnings–accompanied by long-term drug and alcohol abuse, chronic illness, and the internally corrosive effects of despair.

How did the issues of anonymity, accountability, and culpability figure into the legal response to these homicides? All of these women's cases were compromised by the anonymity and lack of accountability that attach to johns and their behavior. Prosecutors and jurors seemed to imagine the encounter as one in which the john was passive, remote, or simply invisible. My sense is that prosecutors and jurors believe that, since johns say they are looking for "impersonal" sex in a prostitution transaction, that johns also *behave* impersonally–meaning *nonaggressively*. Or that they were "personal," but not as johns–instead, they are viewed by juries (as happened in the Aileen Wournos case) as nice, ordinary married men who just happened to have a prostitute in their cars. Thus, when the prostituted women describe these johns as hostile and violent, the women are met with disbelief.

Prostituted women need equal access to self-defense claims. To achieve that goal, it is crucial that advocates articulate the precise behaviors that johns actually display in prostitution transactions as a matter of course and as threats and violence escalate. We have worked hard to give voice to describe how women experience prostitution. But we perhaps still face the task of describing what the men actually *do* to prostituted women–and why, consequently, women sometimes fight back with lethal force. Prosecutors and jurors need to know how often johns make lethal threats or subject prostituted women to deadly force. They need to know the basic dynamics of how lethality risks intensify within a prostitution transaction, and how prostituted women perceive and respond to those dynamics. For domestic violence survivors, "battered women's defenses" similarly explain these life and death patterns as they occur within an on-going relationship. We need to provide the same accounts of the risks faced by prostituted women from men who may be strangers to her but who need not remain anonymous to the law or remain unaccountable for their aggression towards prostitutes.

Now I would like to raise what I think is a more controversial point and one about which I am personally unresolved. I mentioned earlier that the prostituted women I have worked with, who ultimately killed abusers, had all come to an awful point of despair, mental confusion, and internal disintegration by the time the homicide occurred. They were carrying with them terrible, nearly unendurable burdens of all the abuse they had suffered since childhood and over a lifetime. In some way, I do not yet know how to express that each of these johns was made accountable for the abuse they each inflicted on the women as it contributed to the accumulated effect of all the prior abuse that each woman had endured to that point. To what extent *should* a john be held accountable for adding a last, intolerable measure of harm in a woman's life already wounded by the sexual system from which he seeks to benefit? Should a john be held to assume the risk that the woman he buys so casually one night is a woman nearing collapse? In law, we have other examples of individuals being held responsible for a collectively inflicted harm, e.g., in tort under principles of joint and several liability and under environmental compensation rules. I would propose here that we examine closely what kind of accountability is justly attributed to any john who adds his measure of damage to a woman whose resilience and hope ultimately constricts to the vanishing point. I do not know the answer to this question, but I think it deserves our attention.

Prostituted women who have killed johns and pimps are punished severely. As I mentioned earlier, Aileen Wournos was executed last year by lethal injection. Another woman I worked with, convicted of first-degree murder, was sentenced to life with a twenty-five-year mandatory minimum term of incarceration. They bore a heavy weight of culpability for the offenses for which they stood convicted. In the second case, the jury was never even *told* that the woman had been prostituted and pimped by the decedent. As the anonymity of johns is breached, however, and their accountability more closely scrutinized, I am hopeful that prosecutors and jurors can more fairly assess the culpability, whatever that quantum may be, that these women should bear for having taken a life. For the leadership, we should and can provide to others in the legal system who are grappling with these issues, we would do well to explore and illuminate our own view of that question.

At present, I am afraid that the pattern we have heard repeatedly described in this conference–of john anonymity, lack of accountability, and the attribution of sole culpability to prostituted women–holds sway in the prosecution of prostitutes' self-defense claims.

2. *Civil remedies for damages against johns and pimps.* A second strategy for intervening on demand is to provide prostituted women with legal tools to enforce damages claims against johns and pimps. This strategy intervenes on demand in at least two ways: first, the prospect of damages judgments may serve to deter prospective johns from engaging in prostitution, and, second, monetary awards to survivors can assist them in exiting prostitution. I drafted and lobbied for a statute that creates such a legal claim in Florida;[4] the Florida statute was later used as a model for a similar statute passed in Minnesota.[5] Both statutes afford civil damages claims for women coerced in prostitution; in Florida, whether by johns or pimps. Under the Florida law, "coercion" is defined in the statute to include physical force or threat, torture, and kidnapping. Tactics of control exploiting legal and social vulnerabilities of girls and women in prostitution are also actionable, including threats of legal interference with the woman's relationship with her children. In addition, the statute defines as coercive those sexual "bargains" that exploit a woman's isolation, need, and despair. Thus, the statute prohibits inducement to prostitution by:

(k) Restraint of speech or communication with others.
(l) Exploitation of a condition of developmental disability, cognitive limitation, affective disorder, or substance dependency.
(m) Exploitation of victimization by sexual abuse.
(n) Exploitation of pornographic performance.
(o) Exploitation of human needs for food, shelter, safety, or affection.[6]

---

[4]*See* FLA. STAT. 796.09. For a discussion of the statute and its enactment, *see* Margaret A. Baldwin, *Strategies of Connection: Prostitution and Feminist Politics*, 1 MICH. J. OF GENDER & L. 65 (1993).

[5]*See* MINN. STAT. 611A.80 (1994). For a discussion of the scope of the Minnesota law, and its enactment, *see* Evelina Giobbe & Sue Gibel, *Essay: Impressions of a Public Policy Initiative*, 16 HAMLINE J. PUBLIC L. & POL'Y 1 (1994).

[6] FLA. STAT. 796.09(k)-(o).

Taken together, these provisions describe the conditions under which most, if not all, prostitution occurs. The statute affirms that women and girls are not available to be prostituted and do not consent to it by the fact of being human with real needs, real vulnerabilities, and real wounds.

Litigation under the Florida statute has yielded some interesting results in terms of the themes of anonymity, accountability, and culpability that we have been exploring here. As hoped, claims brought under the statute have, I think, successfully created a process for accountability to survivors–especially economic accountability. Of the cases I know of that have been brought under the law, all have resulted in significant financial settlements in favor of the claimants. To the extent that financial commitment denotes accountability for wrongdoing, these settlements seem to meet that equation. In addition, culpability for the woman's prostitution, and its effects, shifts to the johns and pimps when they are sued under the law, rather than resting culpability on the woman. Indeed, some claims under the statute have expanded culpability for economically coercive sex beyond the prostitution framework as we usually encounter it. For example, in one claim a woman successfully sued a car dealership when a salesman predicated a favorable car loan interest rate on the claimant having sex with him.

One reason for this ready economic accountability, it seems, is that the defendants in these cases preferred rapid resolution of the claims to public disclosure of their behavior. In all of the cases I know of, the claims were resolved by confidential settlements containing strong non-disclosure provisions. The concerns motivating these provisions–concerns with retaining anonymity–have been most apparent in the cases falling outside the ambit of prostitution as we usually understand it.[7] The case I just cited involving the car dealership and its salesman is one example; another was a case involving a manager at a family restaurant. In sum, these cases demonstrate an interesting mix of johns' acceptance of accountability and culpability, but with the condition that they remain entitled to anonymity. Thus, while these kinds of civil remedies hold strong promise as avenues of justice for prostituted women,[8] the litigation pattern I just described raises the intriguing

---

[7]The only case under 796.09 that has resulted in a published opinion was a case brought against a brothel. *See Balas v. Ruzzo,* 703 So. 2d 1076 (Fla. App. 1998).

question: why *is* anonymity such a strongly valued entitlement among men who constitute the "demand" for prostitution?

3. *Criminal intervention on johns.* My intuition is that we can begin to understand the stake johns have in anonymity by taking a very close look at the issues entailed in enforcing–or in declining to enforce– criminal sanctions against them. Of course, until relatively recently few states even purported to impose criminal sanctions against johns for prostitution.[9] And modern patterns of enforcement continue the same policy *de facto*. Law enforcement targets prostituted women for arrest and prosecution, rarely arresting johns. When johns are arrested, they are usually released once they provide witness statements incriminating the woman. "Selective enforcement" suits that challenge these arrest patterns as discriminatory have generally failed on the ground that law enforcement's preference for arresting the prostitute rather than the john is legally justified.

The reasoning set out in a 1977 California decision is representative of these cases.[10] First, the court asserts that it is more efficient from the standpoint of crime prevention to arrest prostitutes rather than johns. Describing a "pyramid" of wrong-doers, "[t]he customer forms

---

[8]I therefore am strongly in favor of efforts to reenact the civil cause of action under the Violence Against Women Act, at the federal and at state levels, including prostitution as a basis for claims under its provisions. Indeed, had prostitution been included as a basis for recovery under the statute as initially enacted, the constitutional fortunes of the statute might have been quite different from the outset. *Compare Caminetti v. U.S.*, 242 U.S. 470 (1917) (upholding the constitutionality of the Mann Act, against a Commerce Clause challenge, as applied to both commercial and non-commercial "immoral activities") *with Morrison v. U.S.*, 529 U.S. 598 (2000) (holding civil remedy for gender-based violence exceeded Congress' legislative power under the Commerce Clause).

[9]For example, the Massachusetts prostitution statute, in effect in 1977, criminalized only the conduct of prostitutes, not johns. *See Commonwealth v. King*, (Mass. App. 1977). The court upheld this statute against an equal protection challenge, on the ground that the legislature could rationally distinguish between "sellers" and "buyers" in the allocation of criminal penalties. *Id. See also State v. Wilbur*, 110 wash. 2d 16, 749 P.2d 1295 (1988)(holding that the state prostitution law does not criminalize "patronizing" a prostitute, although it does criminalize "receiving" a fee for sex). Other states, while penalizing both johns and prostituted women, imposed harsher penalties on the prostituted woman. *See, e.g. Commonwealth v. Finnegan*, 421 A.2d 1086 (Pa. Ct. App. 1980)(woman subject to third degree misdemeanor sanction; john guilty only of a "summary offense").

[10]*People v. Superior Court of Alameda County*, 562 P.2d 1315 (Cal. App. 1977).

the base of the triangle, the prostitute. . . constitutes the largest class of profiteers." A "profiteer-oriented" arrest strategy, the court continues, is justified as the most efficient way to utilize law enforcement resources.[11] Second, the court concludes that arresting prostitutes has a greater deterrent effect than arresting johns:

> Prostitutes, the municipal court found, average five customers a night; the average customer does not patronize prostitutes five times a year. Because of an effective grapevine, arrest of one prostitute by an undercover officer will deter others, at least for a time. Customers, on the other hand, are usually unknown to each other. Therefore, in the absence of widespread publicity, arrest of one customer will not deter others.[12]

Third, prostitutes, unlike johns, are often unable to provide adequate identification *bona fides* sufficient under law to qualify them for release on citation. If an arrestee is unable to provide "satisfactory evidence of personal identification," she is subject to custodial arrest, which then triggers an investigation into her family status, residency history, and criminal history. The court noted:

> Between 26 February 1975 and 23 April 1975, 109 female prostitutes were arrested. Of the 109, 20 had no identification or refused to identify themselves, 13 had aliases or suspect identification, 29 had no permanent address, 30 were not permanent residents of the area, 34 had no relatives in the area, 74 were not regularly employed, and 50 had prior arrests or convictions for prostitution. During the same period, 24 male customers were arrested. Of the 24, all had reliable identification, only one had no permanent address, only two were not permanent residents of the area, all were regularly employed, and only one had a prior criminal history indicating that he was a poor citation risk.[13]

---

[11]*Id.* at 1321.

[12]*Id.*

[13]*Id.* at 1322-23.

As if we needed any further convincing, prostitutes and johns are, for all of these reasons, simply not the same for purposes of criminal enforcement policy. This is a maddening opinion and not, as I mentioned before, eccentric in its reasoning. The court makes several assumptions about johns, though, that are instructive for our present discussion of how and why johns want to obscure themselves. The court assumes that johns are the most minor of law-breakers, an assumption that johns would well wish to preserve. The court further assumes that johns participate in prostitution as isolated amateurs, invisible to each other and forming no collective, identifiable social group. Finally, the court gives legal weight to the class (and probably race) privileges that johns typically enjoy, privileges that then ensure that no public arrest record will besmirch them. Committed criminal enforcement of the prostitution laws and related sanctions threaten each of these claims to anonymity–and thus may effectively intervene on demand by deterring johns who wish to avoid disclosure.

A committed law enforcement strategy would demand that johns are charged and prosecuted for the offenses they actually commit in the course of prostitution transactions. The "consumer"/ "profiteer" model is persuasive only if law enforcement continues to look away from the high levels of violence, coercion, insult, and extortion that characterize the actual behavior of johns toward prostituted women. Even when johns are arrested for prostitution, law enforcement officers fail to inquire or investigate whether johns committed these additional crimes against the woman. As a matter of course, law enforcement should begin to inquire whether acts constituting, for example, sexual assault, aggravated battery, attempted murder, kidnapping, stalking, or child sexual abuse, occurred in the course of the transaction. The anonymity of the faceless, harmless "consumer" can be forcefully challenged if assertive investigative protocols like these were adopted by law enforcement.

In addition, the assumption that johns are disconnected, isolated, and infrequent participants in prostitution is belied at any strip club in the country. Strip clubs (along with Internet prostitution sites and sex tourism) link men into markets and into social groups that facilitate prostitution. In strip clubs, men collectively recruit each other into sexually exploitative behavior toward women, including prostitution. Men learn from other men how to treat women in degrading ways, are emboldened by other men to do so themselves, and sometimes are intimidated by other men into compliance with these norms. In effect, strip clubs function as places where men gather to collectively pimp women to other men, self-help style. Again, a committed law enforcement strategy would intervene on these practices and charge men who "solicit, induce, entice or procure another [man] to commit prostitution, lewdness, or assignation" by their behavior in strip clubs under appropriate criminal pimping provisions.[14]

Finally, I want to address the anonymity of class and race privilege. Johns maintain their anonymity through their power to project an image of themselves as stable, employed, "respectable" fellows. For the California court, the fact that a john could present an apparently valid drivers license and a credible home address was enough to satisfy law enforcement that he could be trusted to drive away into the night with no further questions asked (while the prostituted woman would be subject to a custodial arrest and full criminal background check). A john does not have to fear that his family or boss will find out that he was arrested for prostitution, as he might fear if he were arrested along with the woman. His "respectable" identity can remain comfortably intact. Not so, however, if he is subject to car forfeiture penalties, as he might be if he were arrested in Michigan[15] or in a few other jurisdictions.[16] Under the Michigan statute, a vehicle "used for the purpose of lewdness, assignation, or prostitution" is deemed a nuisance,[17] and may be abated by seizure and sale of the vehicle.[18] The cost to a john's anonymity in the event that his car is seized is apparent. His wife, for one, will know that the car has disappeared (and any investment she may

---

[14]The language quoted defines criminal pimping under the Florida prostitution statute. *See* FLA. STAT. ANN. 796.07(2)(f).

[15]MICH. COMP. LAWS ANN. 600.3801, 600.3826 (West 1987).

[16]*See, e.g.* O.C.G.A.16-6-13.2 (2001)(Georgia forfeiture provision, authorizing forfeiture upon conviction of prostitution or for facilitating child prostitution).

[17]MICH. COMP. LAWS ANN. 600.3801.

[18]MICH. COMP. LAWS ANN. 600.3826.

have had in it)[19]–and, ultimately, probably why it disappeared. In addition, the inventory searches of these vehicles, conducted by law enforcement after a car is seized under these kinds of laws, can reveal other secrets in addition to the john's prostitution activity. Any guns, drugs, pornography, or other material the john has in his car will be documented in these searches, eroding the presumption of respectability the john's privilege of anonymity ordinarily affords him. A law enforcement strategy committed to these sanctions would go far toward painting a genuine, reality-based picture of johns' behaviors, while, at the same time, creating a foundation for a more positive alliance between law enforcement and prostituted women and survivors.

I do have a final observation on the import of criminal enforcement of the prostitution laws against johns. The feminist movement has been criticized, and not wrongly, for lacking a strong class and race critique of the criminal justice system as it functions in this country. Specifically, we are criticized for promoting criminal enforcement solutions that strengthen a system that continues to over-prosecute poor and African American men and under-prosecutes white men, while generally overlooking criminal offenses perpetrated against women of color. Enforcing criminal prostitution laws against johns, though, turns that paradigm on its head by focusing enforcement attention (for once) on law-breakers who are predominately white, middle class men who victimize women of color in contexts not far removed from slavery. We have much to learn and much to gain for prostituted women by insisting that the criminal system be accountable to these victims, declare the culpability of these defendants, and remove the mask of anonymity that shields them.

Panel 4: Questions and Answers[20]

[Comment: (Ruth Pojman) There is a lot of evidence that many pimps come from abusive histories themselves. For example, there was

---

[19]*See Bennis v. Michigan*, 116 S. Ct. 994 (1996)(upholding Michigan statute, even as it was applied to deprive an "innocent owner,"-- the john's wife--of her financial interest in the forfeited car).

[20] Bracketed comments are summaries provided by Sara Dubin, Carol Chang, Jamie Sommer, and Rima Kapitan.

an article in the *Washington Post* covering girls in Africa that took up guns after they had been raped. They turned to violence because there were no other resources for dealing with their experiences. We must account for abuse as a form of supply when we discuss the demand of trafficking and prostitution.

Question:(Melissa Farley) Margaret Baldwin's discussion prompted thoughts about when a prisoner of war kills someone in an attempt to escape. Under international law, this act of murder is not construed as homicide. How can this be used to help defend prostitutes who murder their johns?

Answer: (Margaret Baldwin) The model of being held captive can be a useful defense for prostitutes who kill their johns. We must construct the batterer as a jailer. The system that supported his power stood between her and her freedom. She had to gun her way out from her unlawful detainment. We must construct johns as a truly serial presence in her life. If she moves against just one john, she has the chance of attaining her freedom. We must describe prostitution institutionally to show the imagery of a confining reality. The imagery of this confining reality is not communicated if the idea of prostitution is just conveyed as a timeline. Rather, when there is an actionable moment, she is not acting out against the one john present, but more significantly against the series of confinements in her life. This is not communicated as long as prostitution is seen as a timeline in which one person contacts a prostitute at a time without accounting for other confining factors.

Comment: (Norma Hotaling) There are usually no other avenues available to prostitutes to gain their freedom. They are trapped in years of sexual abuse. Every system and institution that they come in contact with victimizes them. They are allowed to be bought again and again. Prostitutes are a group of people that are given free access to be raped, and they are the ones blamed. They rehab themselves by killing a john or becoming a brothel owner.]

PLAN FOR ACTION[1]

Basic Principles

- A focus on demand should be explicit in *every* area.

- Prostituted women must *not* be criminalized; any criminalization of customers and procurers *must* be linked to funding for the provision of support services to prostituted women.

- The distinction between consent and coercion is false in the area of prostitution and sex slavery.

- Violence against women and children will never be abolished without the restructuring of the patriarchal society.

- Child sexual abuse, pornography, prostitution, sexual harassment, domestic violence, rape, trafficking, the sale of children, and the sale of the sex of children are interconnected components that constitute the sex trade and are examples of society's instruction of male entitlement.

Language Development

- Develop a lexicon of words appropriate to describe aspects of sex slavery, including johns, tricks, pimps, etc., which do not indicate endorsement or approval of any aspect of sex slavery and yet adequately describe and name it.

---

[1] Prepared by Morrison Torrey following the Plenary Session discussion; submitted for review and approval to the Conference bulletin board.

- Consider whether the word "trafficking" is one that the average person understands and also takes into account international perspectives; is it now used too broadly?

- Use the active voice to bring the perpetrator into consciousness, *e.g.,* "John beat Mary," rather than the passive voice which focuses on what the victim/survivor endured, *e.g.,* "Mary was beaten by John," which frequently results in "Mary was beaten"–a statement in which the perpetrator disappears.

Education

Societal and Professional Outreach

- Construct a masculinity that respects women and their right to physical safety and sexual autonomy.

- Develop men's action groups based on respecting women and themselves.

- Create a Speakers Bureau and speaking points, including most commonly asked questions and answers about prostitution, sex trafficking, and the sex trade.

- Convince the Advertising Council to develop public service advertisements on sexual slavery.

- Persuade the Association of Treatment of Sex Abusers to integrate issues of "johns" into treatment (note: the Association already does not support pornography).

- Solicit cooperation of the Center on Sex Offender Management to incorporate issues about "johns" in training about sex offenders.

- Encourage all law professors to create and teach classes integrating all aspects of violence against women, including sex slavery.

Police Departments

- Develop model criminal justice policies, legislation, and educational programs for local police departments.

- Provide information on sex trafficking laws to the International Association of Chiefs of Police.

- Convince the National Center for Women in Policing to include information and training about prostitution and sex trafficking (find them at www.feminist.org).

- Create educational programs about sexual slavery for police, prosecutors, and judges.

- Encourage the prosecution of johns and pimps.

- Insist that police and prosecutors enforce criminal laws, such as sexual assault, when prostituted women are the victims of such criminal acts.

Youth Outreach

- Develop a school curriculum program (modeled after the 1980s version of Project Self-Esteem) to teach children about safety from pornography, prostitution, and the affects of violence against women on society as a whole.

- Focus on primary prevention: early enculturation of youth about respect, anger control, and other elements that promote sexual abuse.

Parental Outreach

- Work with schools, churches, and youth groups in teaching parents about the dangers of pornography and prostitution and how to talk to children about these issues.

- Convince fathers that recruiting sons to use prostituted women is harmful to themselves as well as to women.

Legal Reform

International

- Support the 1949 Convention for the Suppression of the Traffic in Persons and of the Exploitation of the Prostitution of Others (found at www.unhchr.ch/html/menu3/b/33.htm).

- Support the Convention on the Elimination of All Forms of Discrimination against Women (CEDAW), Article 6 ["States Parties shall take all appropriate measures including legislation, to suppress all forms of traffic in women and exploitation of prostitution of women."] (the entire Convention can be found at www.un.org/womenwatch/daw/cedaw/cedaw.htm).

- Create World Court and the human rights community's understanding of all forms of violence against women, including prostitution, as a human rights violation.

- Pressure the United Nations to require member nations to pass laws declaring sex with a child, including prostituted children, illegal and punishable with a zero tolerance clause, *i.e.,* "strict liability," that does not require actual knowledge of the child's age.

- Require DNA samples from convicted customers of prostituted women to be maintained in an international database accessible in order to solve other crimes, such as rape.

- Create a centralized database tracking sex trafficking operations.

National

- Lobby for the United States to ratify CEDAW.

- Lobby for language in the Violence Against Women Act (VAWA)[2] to identify prostitution and sex trafficking as violence against women (thus expanding the definition beyond domestic violence, and stalking) *or* define prostitution as a combination of domestic violence, sexual assault, and stalking.

- Lobby for language in the VAWA reauthorization bill refusing funding to any agency that promotes decriminalization or legalization of the use of prostituted women and children.

- Lobby to amend the U.S. Military Code to *zero tolerance* for the solicitation of prostitution by U.S. military personnel and subcontractors.

- Hold U.S. military bases accountable for violence against women and children which is perpetrated by personnel and subcontractors.

- Create a law similar to Amber's Law (in which an "Amber Alert" is issued when a child is kidnapped to be used as a sexual object) for adults who have solicited children for prostitution.

State

- Develop model anti-trafficking legislation at the state level that does not require force or coercion and that can be adapted by any state.

- Adopt a law similar to Sweden's in which prostituted women are not subject to criminal penalties, but customers and procurers are.[3]

---

[2]VAWA was part of an omnibus crime bill, the Violent Crime Control Act of 1994, 108 Stat. 1796, Pub. L. 103-322, and provided a private cause of action for victims to recover damages for gender motivated violence in Sec. 13981, which was subsequently declared unconstitutional in *U.S. v. Morrison*, 529 U.S. 598 (2000). Other provisions were left in tact by the U.S. Supreme Court.

[3]For a discussion of the Swedish law, see Attachment 1.

- Adopt a law similar to Florida's civil restitution tort statue creating a cause of action of prostituted women against procurers and customers.[4]

- Adopt a law similar to Illinois's Gender Violence Act, which provides a civil cause of action for women who have been injured on account of their gender.[5]

- Provide training for tort lawyers about laws allowing women and children to sue their abusers for injuries suffered as a result of sexual violence.

- Convince the criminal justice system, particularly police and prosecutors, to add charges of kidnapping, statutory rape, and child abuse, in order to increase the chances of a conviction and increase the penalty for having sex with a child.

- Target Nevada counties to de-legalize prostitution and to criminalize the purchase of women.

- Lobby for anti-trafficking legislation with a definition broader than the CEDAW Optional Protocol's definition (found at www.un.org/womenwatch/daw/cedaw/protocol/index.html).

Activism

Protests

- Organize coordinated efforts against the Dutch legalization of prostitution.

- Protest at the foreign embassies of states where legalization is being considered.

---

[4]For the text of the statute, see Attachment 2.

[5]For the text of the statue, see Attachment 3.

- Monitor the www.funding.org website to trace and protest anti-abolitionist actions.

- Organize same day (International Women's Day or International Day of No Prostitution or International Day of the Abolition of Slavery) rallies in major U.S. cities protesting demand and at massage parlors, police stations, strip clubs, embassies, tour agencies, etc.

- Crash/protest Exotic/Erotic Balls, pimp conventions, fraternity parties, and any other such gatherings that glorify or mainstream prostitution.

- Picket and handbill strip clubs, pornography shops, "gentlemen's" clubs, massage parlors, publishers, and any other businesses exploiting and expropriating women and children's sexuality.

- Organize "court watches" relating to prostitution prosecutions, including juvenile court; coordinate with domestic violence and sexual assault court watches.

- Attend zoning meetings to protest the issuance of business permits to sex businesses.

Letter Writing

- Send a mass letter (as well as individual letters) to the Board of Directors of the Washington Post and any other newspaper that publishes advertisements of massage parlors and other delivery systems of prostituted women and children.

- Organize a letter writing campaign to the State Department, Department of Defense, Department of Justice, Department of Heath and Human Services, USAID, and all other relevant federal agencies urging them to enforce the federal policy of not funding any organization advocating the legalization of prostitution.

- Write letters to property owners discouraging them from leasing to sex businesses.

Strategic

Continue to Develop an Abolitionist Movement

- Raise men and women's consciousness about sex trafficking and prostitution.

- Reach out to domestic violence and sexual assault communities.

- Unify efforts with coalitions against the trafficking of workers, not to legitimate prostitution as a form of work, but rather to recognize that many women and girls are lured into prostitution by empty promises of other forms of employment.

- Reach out to men's groups, such as SAFE Project and former batterer organizations, in order to encourage a perspective that violence against women is not just a "woman's" problem.

- Consider a celebrity spokesperson and the greater utilization of publicity.

- Create an online forum for partnerships and communication among experts and activists (*e.g.,* list serves, databases, website with current events and developments).

- Establish a REAL "Freedom Network."

- Consider creating a Political Action Committee (PAC) for fund-raising and political action.

Monetary Support

- Create an online forum for funding opportunities and partner-ships.

- Forge more direct relationships with service providers.

- Target donors, foundations, and the government to support anti-sex slavery work and conferences.

Research Agenda

- Analyze the role of religious interpretations and culture in fostering attitudes favorable to sex slavery.

- Determine the impact of race, ethnicity, and class in the prosecution of procurers and customers.

- Obtain federal or private funding for research on customers of sex slavery and how demand is created and maintained.

- Develop a model of violence against women that integrates child sex abuse, pornography, sexual assault, sexual harassment, battering, and prostitution.

Future Conferences

- Hold a forum that deals with how to communicate the issue of sexual slavery, incorporating international perspectives.

- Reach out to all political perspectives, including conservatives, who are potential allies in the Abolitionist Movement.

- Be more global in gathering perspectives on sex slavery, committing to greater diversity in participation.

- Discuss how the Abolitionist Movement can build a coalition to carry out the Action Plan that is united in its focus; develop a name, a mission, and a comprehensive plan.

Attachment 1

Prostitution: "The Oldest Profession in the World - Is It Possible to Reduce Demand?" - *Lisa A. Howard*[6]

I have an American friend who works in an adjoining crystal shop with an exclusive hotel here in Stockholm. She was approached recently while on the job by an average-looking traveling man (staying at the hotel) who asked if she knew where he could find "women." "What?" my friend inquired. "You know, Swedish 'massage parlors' women . . . you know . . ." replied the man. "I *don't* know!" my friend heatedly responded. Is it so difficult to buy sex in Stockholm–even in the inner-city–that he had to ask in a fine crystal shop?

When I met with Gunilla Ekberg (the Special Advisor on issues of prostitution and trafficking in women at the Swedish Division for Gender Equality) recently, I asked if the relatively 'new' tougher legislation on the buying of sexual services is 'working'–*i.e.*, reducing demand of such services–in Sweden. She said, "Look around, did you see any women standing on the streets on your way here?" (Ms. Ekberg's office sits in one of the former most popular districts for prostitutes). And it's true, if you take a look around this capital city, you will be hard-pressed to find women and girls standing on the streets and even fewer brothels and so-called 'Swedish massage parlors.' It is not some kind of illusion that Stockholm has created. The fact that a man had to ask in a fine crystal show for "women" is proof of the success. Actually, I deliver this message to all possible solicitors of sexual services who are planning to travel to Sweden: don't come to Sweden. You will not have success here. "It is a crime to buy sex in Sweden," as the campaign to combat prostitution and trafficking in women by the Regeringskansliet (The Office of the Government of Sweden) proclaims.

"In Sweden, prostitution is regarded as an aspect of male violence against women and children. It is *officially* acknowledged as a

---

[6] Lisa A. Howard is an American criminologist living in Stockholm, Sweden.

form of exploitation of women and children and constitutes a significant social problem, which is harmful not only to the individual prostituted woman or child, but also to society at large," according to the Ministry of Industry, Employment and Communications.[7]

Therefore, in 1999, the Swedish Parliament passed "a law that only criminalized the *buying* of sexual services."[8] Moreover, the new legislation makes it a criminal offense to purchase, or even attempt to purchase, sexual services and is punishable by day fines and/or imprisonment. The women and children, seen as the victims, are not criminalized and will be offered social benefits and advice in an effort to help them "break away" from prostitution or trafficking, giving them alternatives that they previously did not have.[9] To underline Swedish seriousness in matters of these issues, a new law was passed in July 2002 "against trafficking in human rights for sexual purposes . . .this means that all the links in the prostitution and women-trafficking chain have been made a criminal offense in Sweden: the buyers of women and children in prostitution, pimps and traffickers of women." It is essential to understand that "without prostitution, there would be no trafficking in women."[10] Certainly, we can draw the conclusion that without the demand for sexual services, there would be no prostitution.

When considering how to reduce demand for prostitution, a 'root-cause' discussion needs to be brought to the table. Ms. Ekberg states that the root cause of this demand is "men," their demand for women and children. Before putting this article down, consider that statistically speaking, "prostitution is a gender-specific phenomenon; the overwhelming majority of victims are women and girls, while the

---

[7]Regeringskansliet, Fact Sheet April 2003:1 (emphasis added) *Prostitution and trafficking in women.*

[8]Mansson S.A. and Hedin U.C. 1999:68 (emphasis added), *Breaking the Matthew effect - on women leaving prostitution.* International Journal of Social Welfare, 8: 67-77

[9]Ibid., 73; Regeringskansliet, April 2003; Howard L.A. 2001: 14, *Are prostitutes victims of prostitution itself or of the relevant laws and their enforcement?* The University of Edinburgh.

[10] Winberg, 2002:2 Speech by Swedish Deputy Prime Minister Margareta Winberg at the seminar on the effects of legalization of prostitution activities - a critical analysis.

perpetrators are invariably men."[11] To respond to the age-old comment of the pro-legalization movement, "it's the oldest profession in the world," consider this point: "If men did not regard it as their self-evident right to purchase and sexually exploit women and children, prostitution and trafficking would not exist. Human traffickers and pimps profit from women's and girl's economic, social, political, and legal subordination."[12] On this note, consider that the internationally accepted median age for entrance of girls into prostitution is *14* years of age. How many of us believe that the majority of these young girls–children–thought prostitution would be a good career move?

Efforts can be made to reduce the oppression of women by reducing the demand of sexual services. Undeniably, this is not easy to achieve in a patriarchal society. In my conversation with Gunilla Ekberg, she expressed that the Swedish legislation was not developed overnight and much debate took place over a period of years during which people were "questioning men's perceived unlimited sexuality with anyone for the first time." According to Ms. Ekberg, there are three main recommendations that the pro-legislation movement can do to reduce the demand of sexual services in the United States:

- A public debate needs to take place. Open discussions on issues such as the "sexualization" of women, the root causes of prostitution and the effects of a patriarchal society and make visible the men who procure or attempt to procure sexual services (as the typical buyer does not come from the marginalized sector of society).
- Programs for exiting from prostitution need to be developed.
- Educate the enforcers, *i.e.*, the police and the prosecutors.

As a conclusion, the first step to eradicating prostitution is to turn the tide and make it a crime *only* to buy sexual services. Quit punishing the women–the victims–and focus on the demand of such services, extrapolating instead that demand causes supply. The U.S. can only say that it is a democracy when all people are equal and, as long as women are bought and sold as commodities, gender equality will not be

---

[11]Regeringskansliet, Fact Sheet April 2003:2 (emphasis added) *Prostitution and trafficking in women.*

[12]Ibid.

128

achieved. A conference will take place in Chicago October 16-17, 2003, entitled: "Demand Dynamics: The Forces of Demand in Global Sex Trafficking," co-sponsored by DePaul University's International Human Rights Law Institute and Lost Angeles anti-sex trafficking organization Captive Daughters; it is an important initiative to create public awareness in the U.S. about the root causes of prostitution.

Attachment 2

Fla. Stat. § 796.09 (2003)

§ 796.09. Coercion; civil cause of action; evidence; defenses; attorney's fees

(1) A person has a cause of action for compensatory and punitive damages against:

(a) A person who coerced that person into prostitution;

(b) A person who coerces that person to remain in prostitution; or

(c) A person who uses coercion to collect or receive any part of that person's earnings derived from prostitution.

(2) As used in this section, the term "prostitution" has the same meaning as in § 769.07.

(3) As used in this section, the term "coercion " means any practice of domination, restraint, or inducement for the purpose of or with the reasonably foreseeable effect of causing another person to engage in or remain in prostitution or to relinquish earnings derived from prostitution, and includes, but is not limited to:

(a) Physical force or threats of physical force.

(b) Physical or mental torture.

(c) Kidnapping.

(d) Blackmail.

(e) Extortion or claims of indebtedness.

(f) Threat of legal complaint or report of delinquency.

(g) Threat to interfere with parental rights or responsibilities, whether by judicial or administrative action or otherwise.

(h) Promise of legal benefit.

(i) Promise of greater financial rewards.

(j) Promise of marriage.

(k) Restraint of speech or communication with others.

(l) Exploitation of a condition of developmental disability, cognitive limitation, affective disorder, or substance dependency.

(m) Exploitation of victimization by sexual abuse.

(n) Exploitation of pornographic performance.

(o) Exploitation of human needs for food, shelter, safety, or affection.

(4) In the course of litigation under this section, any transaction about which a plaintiff testifies or produces evidence does not subject such plaintiff to criminal prosecution or any penalty or forfeiture. Further, any testimony or evidence, documentary or otherwise, or information directly or indirectly derived from such testimony or evidence which is given or produced by a plaintiff or a witness for a plaintiff shall not be used against these persons in any other investigation or proceeding. Such testimony or evidence, however, may be used against a plaintiff or a witness for a plaintiff upon any criminal investigation or proceeding for perjury committed while giving such testimony or producing such evidence.

(5) It does not constitute a defense to a complaint under this section that:

131

(a) The plaintiff was paid or otherwise compensated for acts of prostitution;

(b) The plaintiff engaged in acts of prostitution prior to any involvement with the defendant; or

(c) The plaintiff made no attempt to escape, flee, or otherwise terminate contact with the defendant.

(6) Evidence of convictions for prostitution or prostitution-related offenses are inadmissible in a proceeding brought under this section for purposes of attacking the plaintiff's credibility.

(7) In any action brought under this section, the court, in its discretion, may award prevailing plaintiffs reasonable attorney's fees and costs.

[There is one reported case to date: *Balas v. Ruzzo*, 703 So. 2d 1076 (Fla. App. 1998).]

Attachment 3

Illinois General Assembly - Full Text of Public Act 093-0416

AN ACT in relation to violence against women.

WHEREAS, Recent national studies demonstrate that women in the United States continue to be greatly harmed by gender-related violence such as domestic violence, which is disproportionately visited upon women by men, and sexual abuse, which harms many women and children without being reported or prosecuted; and

WHEREAS, It is documented that existing State and federal laws have not provided adequate remedies to women survivors of domestic violence and sexual abuse; and

WHEREAS, Women survivors of domestic violence oftentimes have found laws against domestic violence used against them by their batterers; and

WHEREAS, The United States Supreme Court has ruled that the states alone have the authority to grant civil relief to the survivors of such sexually discriminatory violence; and

WHEREAS, Such acts of gender-related violence are a form of sex discrimination; therefore:

Be it enacted by the People of the State of Illinois, represented in the General Assembly:

Section 1. Short title. This Act may be cited as the Gender Violence Act.

Section 5. Definition. In this Act, "gender-related violence," which is a form of sex discrimination, means the following:

(1) One or more acts of violence or physical aggression satisfying the elements of battery under the laws of Illinois that are committed, at least in part, on the basis of a person's sex, whether or not those acts have resulted in criminal charges, prosecution, or conviction.

(2) A physical intrusion or physical invasion of a sexual nature under coercive conditions satisfying the elements of battery under the laws of Illinois, whether or not the act or acts resulted in criminal charges, prosecution, or conviction.

(3) A threat of an act described in item (1) or (2) causing a realistic apprehension that the originator of the threat will commit the act.

Section 10. Cause of action. Any person who has been subjected to gender-related violence as defined in Section 5 may bring a civil action for damages, injunctive relief, or other appropriate relief against a person or persons perpetrating that gender-related violence. For purposes of this Section, "perpetrating" means either personally committing the gender-related violence or personally encouraging or assisting the act or acts of gender-related violence.

Section 15. Relief. In an action brought under this Act, the court may award damages, injunctive relief, or other appropriate relief. The court may award actual damages, damages for emotional distress, or punitive damages. A judgment may also include attorney's fees and costs.

Section 20. Limitation. An action based on gender-related violence as defined in paragraph (1) or (2) of Section 5 must be commenced within 7 years after the cause of action accrued, except that if the person entitled to bring the action was a minor at the time the cause of action accrued, the action must be commenced within 7 years after the person reaches the age of 18. An action based on gender-related violence as defined in paragraph (3) of Section 5 must be commenced within 2 years after the cause of action accrued, except that if the person entitled to bring the action was a minor at the time the cause of action accrued, the action must be commenced within 2 years after the person reaches the age of 18.

Section 98. Applicability. This Act applies only to causes of action accruing on or after its effective date.

Effective Date: 01/01/04

Speaker Biographies

Margaret Baldwin: Professor Baldwin is an associate professor of Law at Florida State University College of Law. Her legal scholarship and advocacy activities have long centered on furthering justice for prostituted women and girls. Professor Baldwin has represented prostituted women in civil rights and clemency cases, authored the first statute in the U.S. creating compensation claims for women and girls coerced into prostitution, and has written extensively on legal strategies benefiting prostituted women and girls.

Michelle Madden Dempsey: Ms. Dempsey is a former criminal prosecutor and civil litigator who is engaged in doctoral research at the University of Oxford regarding the prosecution of violence against women. She has served as a legal and policy consultant to the Crown Prosecution Service of England and Wales, drafted an analysis of the U.S. State Department's Model Trafficking Law on behalf of the Coalition Against Trafficking in Women, and provided legal consultation to the Chicago-based Prostitution Alternatives Roundtable. Ms. Dempsey has lobbied on behalf of Equality Now during the drafting of the U.N. Trafficking Protocol and served as a member of the Violence Reduction Working Group of the Governor's Commission on the Status of Women in Illinois.

Derek Ellerman: Mr. Ellerman is a co-founder and co-executive director of Polaris Project, a Washington, DC-based nonprofit that combats human trafficking. Programs include the Greater DC Community Task Force, the National Trafficking Alert System (NTAS), and HumanTrafficking.com, the world's largest research and activism website on sex trafficking. Recognized as an expert on sex trafficking in the U.S., Mr. Ellerman supervises the development and implementation of Polaris

Project programs. He specializes in victim outreach, community-based investigation, law enforcement collaboration, and trafficking policy. Mr. Ellerman has conducted workshops for the U.S. State Department to help train anti-trafficking professionals from around the world. He founded and, for four years, served as Executive Director of the Center for Police and Community (CPAC), a Providence-based nonprofit working on issues of police reform in Rhode Island. He has also served as president of the Rhode Island Committee for Non-Violence Initiatives, one of most respected non-violence agencies in the state. Mr. Ellerman has a Sc.B. in Cognitive Neuroscience from Brown University, and he is the primary website and graphic designer for PolarisProject.org and HumanTrafficking.com.

Melissa Farley: Dr. Farley brings thirty-five years of practice in clinical psychology to her research on prostitution. She is director of the nonprofit Prostitution, Research & Education (PRE). Dr. Farley has provided consultation to both non-governmental and governmental agencies on prostitution and trafficking. She has published twenty articles in peer-reviewed journals, many on the topic of prostitution. She has just completed editing *Prostitution, Trafficking, & Traumatic Stress,* which will be available this year. In addition to speaking about prostitution at national and international meetings, she has provided testimony on prostitution in forensic cases. She also works with a health research team at Kaiser Permanente, with whom she has published studies delineating the effects of sexual violence on women's health.

Kenneth Franzblau: Mr. Franzblau has worked for Equality Now, an international human rights organization, since 1996. His current work, which focuses on sex tourism, involves finding sex tour companies and gathering information that can be provided to law enforcement and administrative agencies, NGOs, and the media. Mr. Franzblau was previously Equality Now's liaison to the United Nations Human Rights Committee. He has written several op-ed pieces and articles concerning sex tourism and trafficking. Mr. Franzblau holds both a B.A. and M.A. from George Washington University and a J.D. from St. John's University. Before working for Equality Now, he was a labor counsel to numerous police unions in New York State for ten years.

Stephen Grubman-Black: Dr. Grubman-Black, of the University at Buffalo's Department of Speech Communication, holds a joint appointment as Professor of Communicative Disorders and Women's Studies at the University of Rhode Island. Currently coordinator of the Bachelor of General Studies Degree Program and the Academic Advising Program at URI's Alan Shawn Feinstein College of Continuing Education, Dr. Grubman-Black divides his work among administration, teaching, and scholarship. He developed a section of WMS350 (Enforced Silences and Natural Recovery from Childhood Sexual Victimization), which challenges the heterosexist and patriarchal institutions that continue to damage and kill women, girls, and boys. He is the author of *Broken Boys/Mending Men* and offers trainings for professional helpers as well as workshops for male survivors. His current research focus is investigating and challenging the lack of care and regard for disenfranchised and poor victims of male violence.

Kaethe Morris Hoffer: Ms. Morris Hoffer recently co-authored the Gender Violence Act, a groundbreaking civil rights law for survivors of rape and sex-based violence that has been enacted in Illinois and California. She has served on the Governor's Commission on the Status of Women in Illinois, worked as a policy advisor to the Mayor of Chicago, lobbied the U.N. on sex trafficking for Equality Now, directed federal policy for the AIDS Foundation of Chicago, and worked as an attorney for low-income women in Chicago.

Norma Hotaling: Ms. Hotaling is executive director and founder of SAGE (Standing Against Global Exploitation). A former prostitute and heroin addict who spent time in jail, Ms. Hotaling recognizes the underlying connection between trauma, addiction, and prostitution and is committed to the creation of alternatives to homelessness and the incarceration of women and girls. SAGE offers counseling, peer support, drug treatment options, medical treatment, and job training to help women forge a new life. She has designed and implemented model programs that have been adopted internationally, such as the First Offenders Prostitution Program (FOPP), which is for customers of prostitutes and in alliance with the San Francisco District Attorney's Office. Ms. Hotaling, a strong advocate for women and children's rights, has presented internationally and before the U.N. on issues of violence, prostitution, and the sexual exploitation of children. She is the recipient of numerous awards, including Oprah's Angel Award (2001); The Peter F. Drucker Award for Nonprofit Innovation (2000); and the prestigious Innovations in American Government Award (1998). Norma's work has been featured on over 50 television, radio, and print media stories, including *The Oprah Winfrey Show*, *48 Hours*, *Life*, and *The New York Times*.

Kristen Houser: Ms. Houser, a nationally recognized expert on sexual violence, has been working in the movement to end sexual violence for thirteen years. She sits on the board of directors of the National Alliance to End Sexual Violence, is a member of the Violence Against Women Network's Applied Research Forum Advisory Board, and is co-chair of the Rural Issues Committee of the National Task Force to End Sexual and Domestic Violence. She was recently published in the *Sexual Assault Report*, a national publication for professionals who work with survivors of sexual violence and has presented at conferences on sexual and domestic violence across the United States. She has been with the Nebraska Domestic Violence Sexual Assault Coalition since moving to Nebraska in 1998.

Donna Hughes: Dr. Hughes is a professor and holds the Eleanor M. and Oscar M. Carlson Endowed Chair in Women's Studies at the University of Rhode Island. She has been involved in community work, education, and research on violence against women and sexual exploitation for fifteen years. She is an internationally known scholar, researcher, and activist on trafficking of women and girls for prostitution. She has completed research on trafficking for prostitution in the U.S., Russia, and Ukraine. Dr. Hughes was a research consultant to the Council of Europe on the use of new information technologies in the trafficking of women and children for sexual exploitation. She has testified before several congressional hearings and published numerous papers and reports on trafficking and prostitution that are used by researchers and NGO personnel worldwide.

Sandra Hunnicutt: Ms. Hunnicutt is the founding Director of Captive Daughters, the oldest anti-trafficking group in California. Ms. Hunnicutt has seventeen years of nonprofit experience, both salaried and as a volunteer. Sandra's interest in sex trafficking came about when she accompanied her husband on a 94-95 Fulbright teaching grant to Kathmandu, Nepal. Through this visit, Ms. Hunnicutt became aware of the entrenched practice of sex trafficking in Nepal. On returning to the U.S in 1995, she began researching trafficking and found that there was a fragile network of groups educating the public on trafficking both here and abroad. She then established Captive Daughters in Los Angeles in 1997. Prior to founding Captive Daughters, Ms. Hunnicutt was president of Los Angeles Friends of Tibet from 1995-1997 and served six years as executive assistant to the late Dr. Lawrence Towner, President of the Newberry Library in Chicago. Ms. Hunnicutt holds a B.A. in History from the University of Maryland, an M.A.L.S. from Dominican University in Illinois, and an A.A. in merchandising from the Fashion Institute of Design and Merchandising in Los Angeles.

Jackson Katz: Mr. Katz has long been recognized as one of America's leading anti-sexist male activists. In 1993, he founded the Mentors in Violence Prevention (MVP) Program at Northeastern University's Center for the Study of Sport in Society. The multiracial, mixed-gender MVP Program is the first large-scale attempt to enlist high school, collegiate, and professional athletes in the fight against rape and all forms of men's violence against women, and it is the most widely utilized gender violence prevention program in college athletics. In 1996, Katz founded MVP Strategies, which provides gender violence prevention education and training for men and boys in schools, colleges, the U.S. military, and small and large corporations. Since 1996, Mr. Katz has directed the first worldwide gender violence prevention program in the history of the U.S. Marine Corps–the first such program in the U.S. military. From 2000-2003. he served as a member of the U.S. Secretary of Defense's Task Force on Domestic Violence in the military. Mr. Katz is the creator of award-winning educational videos for college and high school students, including "Tough Guise: Violence, Media, and the Crisis in Masculinity," which was named one of the Top Ten Young Adult Videos for 2000 by the American Library Association.

Mary Anne Layden: Dr. Layden is a psychotherapist and Director of Education at the Center for Cognitive Therapy at the University of Pennsylvania. She is the co-director of the Sexual Trauma and Psychopathology Program and the director of the Social Action Committee for Women's Psychological Health. She specializes in the treatment of victims and perpetrators of sexual violence. She has co-authored a chapter with Linnea Smith called, "Adult Survivors of the Child Sexual Exploitation Industry" in Giardino et al. (editors), *Commercial Exploitation of Children: An Experiential Perspective.* She has testified before the U.S. Congress on four occasions, focusing on issues of sexual violence, the sexual exploitation industry, and the media. Dr. Layden has conducted numerous workshops on sexual trauma, sexual addiction, and the sexual exploitation industry.

Laura Lederer: Dr. Lederer currently serves as the senior advisor on Trafficking in the Office of Global Affairs at the U.S. Department of State. She founded the Protection Project at Harvard University in Washington, DC (the project moved to The Johns Hopkins University, School of Advanced International Studies in 2000.) Dr. Lederer served ten years in philanthropy as director of community and social concerns at a private foundation before continuing her education in the law. In 1997, she received the Gustavas Meyers Center for Study of Human Rights Annual Award for Outstanding Work on Human Rights for her work on harmful speech issues. She is the editor of *The Price We Pay: The Case against Racist Speech, Hate Propaganda, and Pornography*, published in 1995, and the author of numerous articles on trafficking, commercial sexual exploitation of women and children, and child pornography.

Dorchen Leidholdt: Ms. Leidholdt is the director of the Center for Battered Women's Legal Services at Sanctuary for Families in New York City, an agency that provides legal representation to battered women in family law, criminal, civil rights, and immigration cases and advocates for policy and legislative changes that further the rights of abused women. An activist and leader in the feminist movement against violence against women since the mid-1970s, Ms. Leidholdt also serves as co-executive director of the Coalition Against Trafficking in Women, an umbrella of grassroots organizations around the world, which she helped found in 1988. Ms. Leidholdt teaches Domestic Violence and the Law at Columbia University School of Law and holds a masters degree from the University of Virginia and a law degree from New York University School of Law. Ms. Leidholdt's writings on sex trafficking include CATW position papers to the U.N. Special Seminar on Trafficking, "Prostitution and the Global Sex Industry," (1999) and

"Prostitution: A Contemporary Form of Slavery", a CATW Presentation to the U.N. Working Group on Contemporary Forms of Slavery.

Mohammed Mattar: Dr. Mattar is an adjunct professor of law and the co-director of the Protection Project at the Johns Hopkins University School of Advanced International Studies in Washington, DC. He is also an adjunct professor of law at Georgetown University Law Center, American University and Washington College of Law. Dr. Mattar's extensive experience and knowledge in the field of international law makes him an authority on the legal and legislative aspects associated with trafficking in women and children. He has written at length on the Trafficking Victims Protection Act of 2000 and the 2000 U.N. Protocol to Prevent, Suppress, and Punish Trafficking in Persons, especially Women and Children. In June of 2002, Dr. Mattar submitted written testimony to the congressional record to the House Committee on International Relations on the 2002 Department of State Trafficking in Persons Report. Dr. Mattar has lectured and participated in numerous panels and conferences related to trafficking in persons. Dr. Mattar received his Doctor of Juridical Sciences in 1986 and Master of Law with Distinction in 1983 from Tulane University School of Law.

Diane L. Rosenfeld: Ms. Rosenfeld currently teaches "Women, Violence and the Law," a Women's Studies course at Harvard College. In 2002, she led "Violence Against Women on the Internet," an online lecture and discussion series. Ms. Rosenfeld recently co-produced with Cambridge Documentary Films a documentary called "Rape Is..." Ms. Rosenfeld formerly served as the Senior Counsel to the Violence Against Women Office at the U.S Department of Justice, where she participated in the implementation of the Violence Against Women Act, both within the Department of Justice and in the various state and federal agencies that are concerned with translating the Act into effective programs. She also served for several years as a legal policy advisor to the Illinois Attorney General, where she specialized in women's advocacy, environmental enforcement, and professional responsibility of government lawyers. Ms. Rosenfeld taught Women and the Law for two years as an Adjunct Professor at the DePaul University College of Law. She received her LL.M. from Harvard Law School, J.D. from the University of Wisconsin Law School, and her B.A. from the University of Illinois.

Vidyamali Samarashinghe: Dr. Samarasinghe is associate professor at American University's School of International Service and lectures frequently on the demand for global sex trade. She teaches and researches gender and development, population and migration issues in developing countries, social science methodology, and field survey methodology. Her regional focus of research is Southeast Asia. She is the co-editor of *Women at the Crossroads: A Sri Lankan Perspective* and *Women at the Center: Gender and Development Issues for the 1990's.*

Pamela Shifman: Ms. Shifman has been researching, writing and speaking about the relationship among gender, sexuality and terrorism for over a decade. An attorney and expert on international women's rights issues, she currently works at UNICEF on a project on sexual exploitation and abuse during humanitarian crises. Ms. Shifman is a former co-executive director of Equality Now, a NY-based international human rights organization for women and a board member of Apne Aap, a grassroots group for women's rights and the eradication of trafficking in women, and Feminist.com, a grassroots, interactive community by, for, and about women. Ms. Shifman holds a law degree from the University of Michigan.

Morrison Torrey: Professor Torrey, an advocate for women's rights, co-founded the Feminist Women Law Teachers Colloquium and developed one of the first seminars in the country on feminist jurisprudence. She also created the DePaul Clemency Project for Battered Women, an innovative program matching students with recent DePaul law graduates to represent incarcerated battered women in clemency proceedings. More recently, she has established The Louise Project for Social Justice, which partners law faculty, staff, alumna, and students with a neighborhood high school in a variety of programs. She is the co-author of one of the most widely adopted casebooks on feminist jurisprudence, *Taking Women Seriously* (2d edition, West 2001). Professor Torrey has written extensively on violence against women and the impact of legal education on women and minorities. Before coming to DePaul Law School in 1987, she practiced in the areas of public and private sector labor law and litigation for the government, a private firm, and a corporate law department.

Marisa Ugarte: Ms. Ugarte, the executive director of the Bilateral Safety Corridor Coalition of San Diego, California, has more than twenty years of experience in advocacy for exploited children and in assisting children and high-risk youth. She spent the past three years creating organizational programs for Tijuana, Mexico. She created the Binational Crisis Line in Tijuana, as well as the Domestic Violence Crisis Center for DIF. Ms. Ugarte is an advisor to DIF and to the Civil Protection in Disaster Crisis Prevention Program. In the U.S., Ms. Ugarte has convened three anti-trafficking conferences and is an active speaker at similar conferences in the U.S. and Central America. Ms. Ugarte taught a masters degree-level module of Crisis Intervention at the University of Xochicalco, Mexico. An alumnus of San Francisco College for Women/USD and Dunbarton University, Washington, DC, she holds an M.A. in social work and psychology.

Conference Participants

Ms. Erin Abrams
Students Organized for the Prevention of Domestic Violence
(STOPDV)
Harvard Law School
c/o Ms. Karen Paik, President,
STOPDV
Story Hall, Room 20
Cambridge, MA 02138
eabrams@law.harvard.edu

Ms. Kirsi Ayre
7133 Mockingbird Way
Anaheim Hills, CA 92807
714-281-8148
kirsi_ayre@yahoo.com

Prof. Margaret Baldwin, Esq.
College of Law, F.S.U.
Tallahassee, FL 32306
850-644-3449
mbaldwin@law.fsu.edu

**M. Cherif Bassiouni, LL.B.,
J.D., LL.M., S.J.D., LL.D.**
President, IHRLI
DePaul University College of
Law
25 E. Jackson Boulevard
Chicago, IL 60604
312-362-8332
cbassiou@depaul.edu
www.law.depaul.edu/ihrli

Ms. Karin Brandenburg
Human Trafficking Coordinator
American Bar Association
Central Eastern & Eurasian
Law Initiative
740 15th Street, NW - 8th Flr
Washington, DC 20005
202-662-1514
kbrandenburg@abaceeli.org

Ms. Susan Breault
Paul & Lisa Program
P.O. Box 348
Westbrook, CT 06498
860-767-7660
susan@paulandlisa.org
www.paulandlisa.org

Mr. Les Brown
Director of Policy
Chicago Coalition for the Homeless
1325 S. Wabash, Suite 205
Chicago, IL 60605
312-435-4548
les@chicagohomeless.org
www.chicagohomeless.org

Twiss Butler, Esq.
National Organization for Women
223 Princess Street
Alexandria, VA 22314
pbutler2@bellatlantic.net

Mr. Tommy Calvert, Jr.
Chief of External Operations
American Anti-Slavery Group
198 Tremont Street - #421
Boston, MA 02116
617-426-8161; 1-800-884-0719
tc@iabolish.com
www.iabolish.com

Michelle Madden Dempsey, Esq.
University of Oxford, New College
Holywell Street
Oxford OX1 3BN
UNITED KINGDOM
(44) 77 66 413 010
michelle@mmdconsulting.net

Ms. Sara Dubin
Northwestern University
121 W. Chestnut, #1006
Chicago, IL 60610
847-708-7016
sbd228@hecky.it.northwestern.edu

Mr. Derek Ellerman
Co-Executive Director
Polaris Project
433 New Jersey Avenue, S.E.
Washington, DC 20003
202-547-7909
dellerman@polarisproject.org

Dr. Melissa Farley
Prostitution Research
P.O. Box 16254
San Francisco, CA 94116
415-922-4555
mfarley@prostitutionresearch.com
www.prostitutionresearch.com

Kenneth Franzblau, Esq.
Equality Now
149 First Street
Nyack, NY 10960
kenjf57@yahoo.com
www.equalitynow.org

Mr. Adam Freer
The Salvation Army
P.O. Box 269
Alexandria, VA 22313
703-684-5150
adam_freer@usn.salvationarmy.
org
www.iast.net

Dr. Stephen D. Grubman-Black
University of Rhode Island
Roosevelt Hall 314/90 Lower
College Road
Kingston, RI 02881
401-874-7066
shalom@uri.edu

David Guinn, J.D., Ph.D.
Executive Director, IHRLI
DePaul College of Law
25 E. Jackson Boulevard
Chicago, IL 60604
312-362-8135
dguinn@depaul.edu
www.ihrli.org

Ms. Teresa Hintzke
President, Chicago Chapter
Pan Pacific & SE Asia
Women's Association
418 Maple
Winnetka, IL 60093
hintzke@cs.com

Kaethe Morris Hoffer, Esq.
1507 Lake Street
Evanston, IL 60201
847-328-2765
morrishoffer@ameritech.net

Ms. Norma Hotaling
Executive Director, The SAGE
Project
1275 Mission Street
San Francisco, CA 94103
415-905-5050
nhsage@sbcglobal.net
www.sageprojectinc.org

Ms. Kristen Houser
Director of Programming, Neb.
Domestic Violence Sexual
Assault Coalition
825 M Street, Suite 404
Lincoln, NE 68508
402-476-6256
khouser@ndvsac.org
www.ndvsac.org
www.prostitutionrecovery.org

Dr. Donna Hughes
University of Rhode Island
6510 Putnam Avenue
Thurmont, MD 21788
301-898-9471
dhughes@uri.edu
www.uri.rdu/artsci/wms/Hughes

Ms. Sandra Hunnicutt
Executive Director, Captive
Daughters
10410 Palms Boulevard - PMB 22
Los Angeles, CA 90034
310-815-1511
captivedaughters@earthlink.net
www.captivedaughters.org

Ms. Margaret Iha
304 N. Cuyler
Oak Park, IL 60302
708-445-0191
biha@earthlink.net

Mr. Jackson Katz, Ed.M
Director, MVP Strategies
3860 Brayton Avenue
Long Beach, CA 90807
562-997-3953
jacksonkatz@aol.com
www.jacksonkatz.com

Ms. Lisa Kelly
Writer, Captive Daughters
10410 Palms Boulevard - PMB
22
Los Angeles, CA 90034
818- 881-3346
bhakti_lk@yahoo.com
www.captivedaughters.org

Mr. Andy Kim
Chicago Coalition for the
Homeless
Prostitution Alternatives
Roundtable
1325 S. Wabash - Suite 205
Chicago, IL 60605
312-435-4548
andykim@uchicago.edu
www.chicagohomeless.org

Ms. Paula Kirlin
Captive Daughters
201 Glenwood Circle, Apt.
36B
Monterey, CA 93940
562-997-3953
peacelovepaula@yahoo.com

Barbara C. Kryszko, Esq.
Coalition Against Trafficking
in Women
123 7th Avenue, #133
Brooklyn, NY 11215
917/749-5479; 212/349-6009,
ext. 249
barbara@catwinternational.org
www.catwinternational.org

Dr. Mary Ann Layden
University of PA Health System
Department of Psychiatry
3535 Market Street – Rm 2023
Philadelphia, PA 19104-3309
215-898-4106
layden@mail.med.upenn.edu

Laura Lederer, Esq.
Senior Advisor on Trafficking
Office of Global Affairs, U.S.
Dept. of State
2201 C Street, NW - Room 7250
Washington, DC 20520
202-647-2990
ledererlj@state.gov

Dorchen Leidholdt, Esq.
Director, Center for Battered
Women
Legal Services
Sanctuary for Families
PO Box 1406
Wall Street Station
New York, NY 10268-1406
DORCHEN@SSFNY.ORG
(Fax) 212-566-0344

Mr. Jon Lindsay
ECPAT USA
157 Montague Street
Brooklyn, NY 11201
718-935-9173
jlindsay@ecpatusa.org
www.ecpatusa.org

Marsha Liss, Esq.
Advisor Attorney, U.S. Dept. of
State
Washington, DC
202-312-9647
lissmb@state.gov

Mr. Stephen Long
Board of Directors, Captive
Daughters
10410 Palms Boulevard –
PMB 22
Los Angeles, CA 90034
213-804-3651
keliinoe@yahoo.com
www.captivedaughters.org

Dr. Mohamed Y. Mattar
The Johns Hopkins University
Protection Project - Suite 515
1717 Massachusetts Ave. NW
Washington, DC 20036
202-663-5887
mmattar@jhu.edu
www.protectionproject.org

Ms. Gayle McCoy
200 S. Michigan - Suite 710
Chicago, IL
312-212-9500, ext. 113; 312-250-0047

Meredith McGowan, Esq.
Sanctuary for Families
Center for Battered Women
Legal Services
67 Wall Street - Suite 2211
New York City, NY 10005
718-993-5990, ext. 32
meredith@sffny.org

Ms. Heena Musabji
DePaul University College of
Law
25 E. Jackson
Chicago, IL 60604
312-362-5919
heenam@comcast.net

Ms. Brenda Myers
Chicago Coalition for the Homeless
1325 S. Wabash, Suite 205
Chicago, IL 60605
312-435-4548
bmyers@chicagohomeless.org
www.chicagohomeless.org

Sister Helen Petrimoulx
165 E. Oak Avenue
Windsor, Ontario, N9A 5E5
CANADA
oaksis@mnsi.net

Ms. Terry Phillips
Soroptimist Club
2727 N. Whipple
Chicago, IL 60647
773-276-2268
fabric@earthlink.net
www.soroptimist.org

Mr. John Picarelli
Transnational Crime and Corruption Center
American University – 240
Nebraska Hall
4400 Massachusetts Ave. NW
Washington, DC 20016-8178
202-885-2657
pic@american.edu
www.american.edu/academic.d
epts/acainst/transcrime

Mr. Jesse Pierce
Illinois Coalition Against Sexual Assault
100 N. 16th Street
Springfield, IL 62703
(217) 753-4117
jpierce@icasa.org
www.icasa.org

Ms. Ruth Pojman
Anti-Trafficking Advisor,
USAID
Ronald Reagan Building
Washington, DC 20523-1000
202-712-0623
rjpojman@usaid.gov

Diane Rosenfeld, Esq.
Women's Studies, Harvard University
2400 Massachusetts Ave.
Lexington, MA 02421
781-424-8939
rosenfel@law.harvard.edu
www.rapeis.org

Dr. Ann Russo
Women's & Gender Studies Program
DePaul University
2219 N. Kenmore Avenue
Chicago, IL 60614-3504
773-325-4086
arusso@depaul.edu

Dr. Vidya Samarasinghe
School of International Service
American University
4400 Massachusetts Ave. NW
Washington, DC 20016
202-885-1487
svidy@american.edu
www.american.edu/sis/faculty/sa
marasinghe

Pamela Shifman, Esq.
UNICEF
Prevention of Sexual Exploitation & Abuse in Humanitarian Crises
3 United Nations Plaza
New York City, NY 10017
pshifman@unicef.org

Dr. Linnea Smith
LWS Psychiatry
105 Fox Run
Chapel Hill, NC 27516
919-968-1982
linnea@mindspring.com

Ms. Lisa Thompson
National Consultant for Youth Development
Liaison for Sexual Trafficking Project
The Salvation Army
P.O. Box 269
Alexandria, VA 22313
703-519-5896
Lisa_Thompson@usn.salvationarmy.org
www.iast.net

Morrison Torrey, Esq.
DePaul College of Law
25 E. Jackson Boulevard
Chicago, IL 60604
312-362-8135
mtorrey@depaul.edu

Ms. Marina Trebukhina
645 Congress Street - #32
Portland, ME 04101
207-228-8711
marina.trebukhina@maine.edu

Ms. Marisa Ugarte
Exec. Dir., Bilateral Safety Corridor Coalition
5348 University Avenue - St. 119
San Diego, CA 92105
619-265-0105
mubava@msn.net
www.bsccoalition.org

Mr. Steven Wagner
Senior Consultant, Admin. for Children & Families
Trafficking in Persons Program
901 D Street SW, Suite 600 West
Washington, DC 20447
202-260-1853
swagner@acf.hhs.gov

Yosh Yamanaka, Esq.
Board of Directors, Captive Daughters
10410 Palms Blvd - PMB 22
Los Angeles, CA 90034
310-227-6107
globaljustice@attbi.com
www.captivedaughters.org

Ms. Mira Binti Yusef
Asian Coalition Against Domestic Violence & Sexual Assault
2603 Bell Avenue
Des Moines, IA 50321
515-244-7424
acadvsa@earthlink.net

Ms. Hanna Zylberberg
Board of Directors, Captive Daughters
10410 Palms Boulevard - PMB 22
Los Angeles, CA 90034
310-315-0531
hannazyl@msn.com
www.captivedaughters.or

Conference Supporters

Ms. Gunilla Ekberg
Trafficking Advisor & Director of Sweden's
Campaign Against Prostitution
Stockholm, Sweden

Dr. Juliette Engel
Miramed
Moscow, Russia

Dr. Annalisa Enrile
U.C.L.A. & Gabriela USA
Los Angeles, CA

Mr. Matthew S. Friedman
Bangkok, Thailand

Mr. Samir Goswami
Chicago Coalition for the
Homeless
Chicago, IL

Mr. Joseph Grieboski
Institute for Religion & Public
Policy
Washington, DC

Ms. Ruchira Gupta
Washington, DC

Mr. Bruce Harris
Casa Alianza, Costa Rica

Dr. Anele Heiges, O.P.
International Public Policy
Institute
New York City, NY

Ms. Jeanette Heinrichs
University of Pittsburgh
Pittsburgh, PA

Ms. Alyssa Leal
Captive Daughters
Los Angeles, CA

Ms. Meghan McCleary
Washington, DC

Noah Novogrodsky, Esq.
University of Toronto, College
of Law
Toronto, Ontario, Canada

Ms. Connie Oxford
University of Pittsburgh
Pittsburgh, PA

Diane Post, Esq.
Arizona Coalition Against
Domestic Violence
Phoenix, AZ

Dr. Jody Raphael
Impact Research
Chicago, IL

Dr. Janice Raymond
Coalition Against the Trafficking of Women

North Amherst, MA
Amb. Ellen Sauerbrey
U.S. Representative to the
U.N. Commission
on the Status of Women
Washington, DC

Ms. Leslie Wolfe
Center for Women's Policy
Studies
Washington, DC

Postscript

Captive Daughters and DePaul's International Human Rights Law Institute are already in the planning stages for a follow-up conference, "Pornography and Its Role in Creating and Maintaining Demand for Global Sex Trade," to be held in October of 2004. If you wish to participate, please contact us at DDChicago2004@yahoo.com or Captive Daughters, 10410 Palms Blvd, PMB 22, Los Angeles, CA 90034.

Bibliography: Demand in Global Sex Trafficking

Compiled by Heena Musabji

1. Banarjee, Upalla Devi. Sexual Exploitation and Trafficking of the Girl Child: The Indian Scenario. Global March. <http://www.globalmarch.org/child_labour_today/sexual_exp.php 3>

2. Barry, Kathleen. Female Sexual Slavery. New York: NYU Press, 1979.

3. Barry, Kathleen. The Prostitution of Sexuality. New York: NYU Press, 1995.

4. Briere, J. and Runtz, M. "University Males' Sexual Interest in Children: Predicting Potential Indices of Pedophilia in a Nonforensic Sample." Child Abuse and Neglect. 1989; 13(1): 65-75.

5. Brooks, PhD., Gary R., The Centerfold Syndrome: How Men Can Overcome Objectification and Achieve Intimacy with Women, San Fransisco: Josey-Bass Publishers, 1995.

6. Bryant, Jennings. Testimony to the Attorney General's Commission on Pornography. Houston, Texas. Hearing. 1985: 128-57.

7. Check, J. "Teenage Training: The Effects of Pornography on Adolescent Males." In: Lederer, L. and Delgado, R., eds. The Price We

Pay: The Case Against Racist Speech, Hate Propaganda and Pornography. New York: Hill and Wang; 1995: 89-91.

8. "Child Prostitution; Curb Sex Slavery by Reducing Demand," The San Diego Union-Tribune. 9 Dec 2001.

9. Combating Trafficking of Women and Children in South Asia: Guide for Integrating Concerns into ADB Operations, Asian Development Bank, Apr 2003, <http://www.adb.org/Documents/Guidelines/Combating_Trafficking/Guide_Integrating_Trafficking_Concerns.pdf>.

10. Committee on Public Education, American Academy of Pediatrics. "Sexuality, Contraception, and the Media." Pediatrics. 2001; 107(1): 191-194.

11. Corne, S. and Briere, J. Journal of Interpersonal Violence. 1992; 7(4): 454-461.

12. Cotton, Ann, Farley, Melissa & Baron, Robert (2002). "Attitudes toward Prostitution and Acceptance of Rape Myths". Journal of Applied Social Psychology 32 (9): 1790-1796.

13. Cotton, Ann, Farley, Melissa, & Schmidt, Megan (2001) "Prostitution Myth Acceptance, Sexual Violence, and Pornography Use." Presentation at Annual Meeting of the American Psychological Association, San Francisco CA. 27 Aug 2001.

14. Davidson, Julia O'Connell. The Sex Exploiter: Theme Paper for the World Congress Against the Commercial Sexual Exploitation of Children, U.S Embassy Stockholm, 27-31 Aug 1996, <http://www.usis.usemb.se/children/csec/the_sex_exploiter.html>.

15. Ekberg, Gunilla. (2003). Final Report. Nordic-Baltic Campaign against Trafficking in Women, 2002. Nordic Council of Ministers. See especially pp. 30-35; 69-79. <http://nordicbaltic campaign.org>.

16. Estes, Richard J., and Neil Alan Weiner, "The Commercial Sexual Exploitation of Children to the U.S, Canada and Mexico", U of Penn. 18 Sept 2001 (amended Apr. 2002), <http://caster.ssw.upenn.edu/~restes/CSEC_Files/Complete_CSEC _020220.pdf>.

17. Fact Sheet from Swedish Government Offices. (1998). Violence Against Women, Government Bill 1997/98:55. English summary of the Swedish Law prohibiting the purchase of sexual services. www.kvinnofrid.gov.se

18. Factors that Contribute to the Trafficking of Women, Stop Violence Against Women, Minnesota Advocates of Human Rights, <http://www1.umn.edu/humanrts/svaw/trafficking/explore/3factors .htm>.

19. Farley, Melissa (2003) "Johns: prostituted women's accounts, social science anecdotes, but little research." Panel Presentation Prostitution: a Perspective on the customer's domination of women. 111th Annual Meeting of the American Psychological Association. Toronto, Canada, 28 Aug 2003.

20. Farley, M., Becker, T., Cotton, A., Sawyer, S., Fitzgerald, L., & Jensen, R. (1998) "The Attitudes toward Prostitution Scale: College Students' Responses Compared to Responses of Arrested Johns." 14th Annual Meeting of the International Society for Traumatic Stress Studies, Washington, D.C., 21 Nov 1998.

21. Government of Sweden Web Site. Documents on National Swedish Campaign on Prostitution and Trafficking, Limited availability in English. http://naring.regeringen.se/fragor/jamstalldhet/kvinnohandel/kamp anj.htm

22. Hotaling, Norma and Leslie Levitas-Martin, Increased demand Resulting in the Flourishing Recruitment and Trafficking of Women and Girls: Relating Child Sexual Abuse and Violence Against Women, 13 HASTINGS WOMEN'S L.J. 117, (2002).

23. Hughes, Donna M, "Pimps and Predators on the Internet: Globalizing the Sexual Exploitation of Women and Children", The Coalition Against Trafficking in Women. U of R.I., (1999), <http://www.uri.edu/artsci/wms/hughes/pprep.pdf>.

24. Hughes, Donna M., "The Demand: The Driving Force of Sex Trafficking", The Human Rights Challenge of Globalization in Asia-Pacific U.S.: The Trafficking in Persons Especially Women and Children, Globalization Research Center, U of Haw., 14 Nov 2002. Paper Presentation. <http://www.uri.edu/artsci/wms/hughes/the_demand>.

25. Hughes, Donna M., "Men Create the Demand; Women are the Supply", Lecture on Sexual Exploitation. Valencia, Spain, Nov 2002, <http://www.uri.edu/artsci/wms/hughes/demand.htm>.

26. Hughes, Donna. "The Impact of the Use of New Communications and Information Technologies on Trafficking in Human Beings for Sexual Exploitation: A Study of the Users". Committee for Equality Between Men and Women, May 2001. <http://www.uri.edu/artsci/wms/hughes/study_of_users>.

27. Hughes, Donna. "The World's Sex Slaves Need Liberation, Not Condoms," The Weekly Standard. 21 Feb 2003.

28. Hynes, Patricia and Raymond, Janice G. Put in Harm's Way: The Neglected Health Consequences of Sex Trafficking in the United States, Policing the National Body: Sex, Race and Criminalization, 31 Jul 2002, <http://action.web.ca/home/catw/attach/Put%20in%20Harm%5C%27s%20Way3.doc>.

29. Itzin, Catherine. "Pornography and the Organization of Intra- and Extrafamilial Child Sexual Abuse in Kantor." In: Glenda Kaufman & Jasinski, Jana L., Out of Darkness: Contemporary Perspectives on Family Violence, Sage Publications, California, 1992.

30. Jeffreys, Sheila. The Idea of Prostitution. North Melbourne, Australia: Spinifex Press, 1997.

31. Katz, J. "Advertising and the Construction of Violent White Masculinity: From Eminem to Clinique for Men". In Gail Dines and Jean Humez, Gender, Race and Class in Media, CA: Sage, 2002.

32. Kouvo, Sari. "The Swedish Approach to Prostitution", Dept. of Law, University of Goteborg, Sweden, <http://www.penelopes.org/Anglais/xarticle.php3?id_article=21>.

33. Loviglio, Joann. "Researchers: Go After Adults who abuse kids, not the children," Associated Press. 4 Dec 2001.

34. Malamuth, N. "New Research on the Harm of Pornography." Speech, Equality and Harm Conference, University of Chicago Law School. March 7, 1993.

35. Mansson. Sven-Axel. (2002). "Why Do Men Buy Sex?" NIKK Magasin (Nordic Institute for Women's Studies and Gender Research), 1: pp. 22-25. Available at <nikk@nikk.uio.no>

36. Marshall, W.L. "Pornography and Sex Offenders." In: Zillman, Dolf and Bryant, J., eds. Pornography: Research Advances and Policy Considerations. Hillsdale, New Jersey: Lawrence Erlbaum; 1989: 203-10.

37. Phinney, Alison. "Trafficking of Women and Children for Sexual Exploitation in the America's." Inter-American Comission of Women and the Women, Health and Development Program, February 2002., <http://www.planetwire.org/wrap/files.fcgi/2369_trafficking_paper.htm>.

38. Raphael, Jody and Deborah L. Shapiro. Sisters Speak Out: The Lives and Needs of Prostituted Women in Chicago, A Research Study. Center for Impact Research, Aug. 2002. <http://www.impactresearch.org/documents/sistersspeakout.pdf>.

39. Raymond, Janice G. "10 Reasons for Not Legalizing Prostitution." 2003, Available at <www.catwinternational.org>

40. Raymond, J., Hughes, D. and Gomez, C. Sex Trafficking of Women in the United States: Links Between International and Domestic Sex Industries, Funded by the U.S. National Institute of Justice. N. Amherst, MA: Coalition Against Trafficking in Women. 2001, Available at <www.catwinternational.org>.

41. Raymond, J., d'Cunha, J., Ruhaini Dzuhayatin, S., Hynes, H.P., Ramirez Rodriguez, Z., and Santos, A. A Comparative Study of Women Trafficked in the Migration Process: Patterns, Profiles and Health Consequences of Sexual Exploitation in Five Countries (Indonesia, the Philippines, Thailand, Venezuela and the United States). Funded by the Ford Foundation. N. Amherst, MA: Coalition Against Trafficking in Women (CATW). 2002, Available at <www.catwinternational.org>.

42. Richard, Amy O'Neill. "International Trafficking in Women to the United States: A Contemporary Manifestation of Slavery and Organized Crime", Center for the Study of Intelligence, U.S. Department of Justice. Apr 2002, <http://www.ncjrs.org/pdffiles1/nij/trafficking.pdf>.

43. Rudman, L.A., Borgida, E. "The Afterglow of Construct Accessibility: The Behavioral Consequences of Priming Men to View Women as Sexual Objects." Journal of Experimental Social Psychology. 1995; 31:493-517.

44. Schmidt, M., Cotton, A & Farley, M. (2000) "Men's Attitudes toward Prostitution and Self-Reported Sexual Violence." Presentation at the 16th Annual Meeting of the International Society for Traumatic Stress Studies, San Antonio, Texas, 18 Nov 2000.

45. The Second World Congress on the Commercial Sexual Exploitation of Children, U.S. Gov. Report, Yokohama, Japan, 17-20 Dec. 2001, <http://www.usdoj.gov/criminal/ceos/2ndWrldCong.pdf>.

46. Sex Slaves: Trafficking in Human Beings from Moldova to Italy, British Helsinki Human Rights Group,

<http://www.bhhrg.org/CountryReport.asp?ReportID=160&Countr yID=16>.

47. Silbert, Mimi H. and Ayala M. Pines, "Pornography and Sexual Abuse of Women," Sex Roles, 10 (1984): 857-868.

48. The Trafficking Project & Articles, Stiftelten Kvivvonoforum. Available at <http://www.qweb.kvinnoforum.se/>.

49. Villani, Susan, MD. "Impact of Media on Children and Adolescents: A 10-Year Review of Research." J. Am. Acad. Child Adolesc. Psychiatry. 2001; 40(4): 392-401.

50. Warburton, Jane. Theme Paper for the Second World Congress Against Commercial Sexual Exploitation of Children: Prevention, Protection and Recovery, Yokohama, Japan, 2001. <http://www.mofa.go.jp/policy/human/child/congress01-r.html>.

51. Willis, Brian M., Levy, Barry S. "Child Prostitution: Global Health Burden, Research Needs, and Interventions." The Lancet. 2002; 359: 1417-1422.

52. Wilson, Onnie. "Globalized Female Slavery." Said it: Feminist News, Culture and Politics. April 2002. <http://www.prostitutionresearch.com/wilson-trafficking.html>

53. Wingood, Gina M., ScD, MPH, DiClemente, Ralph J., PhD, Harrington, Kathy, MPH, Davies, Suzy, DrPH, MPH, Hook, Edward W., III, MD, Oh, M. Kim, MD. "Exposure to X-rated Movies and Adolescents' Sexual and Contraceptive-Related Attitudes and Behaviors." Pediatrics. 2001; 107: 1116-1119.

54. Wyre, R., "Pornography and Sexual Violence: Working with Sex Offenders." In: Itzin, Catherine, Pornography: Women, Violence and Civil Liberties, Oxford: Oxford University Press, 1992.

55. Zillman, Dolf. "Effects of Prolonged Consumption of Pornography." In: Zillmann, Dolf and Bryant, J., eds. Pornography: Re-

search Advances and Policy Considerations. Hilsdale, New Jersey: Lawrence Erlbaum; 1989: 147.

56. Zillmann, Dolf, Bryant, Jennings, Huston, Aletha C., eds. Media, Children, and the Family: Social Scientific, Psychodynamic, and Clinical Perspectives. Lawrence Erlbaum Associates, Inc. Hillsdale, New Jersey, 1994.